MAL LOR CA

T0001491

Travel with Marco Polo
Insider Tips

INSIDER TIP
Your shortcut
to a great
experience

MARCO POLO
TOP HIGHLIGHTS

BANYALBUFAR/ ESTELLENCS ⭐

You will get fit going up and down the steps in these two pretty terraced villages in the west (photo).

➤ p. 65, The West

SÓLLER VALLEY ⭐

It's hard to imagine a more beautiful landscape. Set among high mountains, it is an unbeatable place to go hiking.

📷 *Tip: Take the steps up to Biniaraix on the left as you come into the village to get a photo of one of the most beautiful narrow streets on Mallorca.*

➤ p. 69, The West

TORRENT DE PAREIS ⭐

There are plenty of ways to get to Europe's second biggest canyon. For a relaxed approach, take the boat or drive; the more adventurous will walk.

➤ p. 72, The West

FORMENTOR PENINSULA ⭐

Enjoy sensational views of rocky cliffs and a deep-blue sea from the viewpoint Es Colomer. Then watch the sunset from Talaia d'Albercutx.

📷 *Tip: Wait until the sun has dropped below the horizon for an explosion of reds, oranges and yellows across the sea.*

➤ p. 92, The North

ES TRENC/PLATJA DE SA RÀPITA ⭐

Two for the price of one! Two of best beaches on the island are right next to each other and are so perfect you'll think you're in the Caribbean.

➤ p. 113, The South

LA SEU 8

Climb up to the roof of Palma's magisterial masterpiece of a cathedral. The "Terraces Tour" allows you access to areas that have been sealed off for centuries.
📷 *Tip: Don't miss the views down to the sea from the southern terraces.*

➤ p. 42, In & Around Palma

GRAN HOTEL 9

The best of art nouveau, with an exhibition by the painter Anglada Camarasa inside and a perfect position on the Plaça Weyler outside.
📷 *Tip: Get down on one knee! To get an unusual and beautiful view of the building, get down as low as you can.*

➤ p. 45, In & Around Palma

PUIG DE RANDA 6

The holy mountain in the middle of the island is home to three large monasteries and a wealth of gastronomic treats at almost heavenly altitudes.

➤ p. 129, The Centre

ELS CALDERERS 7

Pay a visit to this fascinating ancient estate.
📷 *Tip: Find an unusual angle on the lavishly decked table for a great photo.*

➤ p. 131, The Centre

PORT DE PORTALS 10

Chic marina with posh boutiques and exclusive restaurants, this is Mallorca's luxurious answer to Marbella. For people who like to be seen to be living the high life.

➤ p. 55, In & Around Palma

CONTENTS

THE WEST
THE NORTH
IN & AROUND PALMA
THE CENTRE
THE EAST
THE SOUTH

CONTENTS

☉	Plan your visit	🍴 Eating/drinking	🛉 Rainy day activities
€–€€€	Price categories	🛍 Shopping	🐗 Budget activities
(*)	Premium rate phone number	🍸 Going out	👥 Family activities
		🌴 Top beaches	🚩 Classic experiences

(🕮 A2) Refers to the removable pull-out map
(🕮 a2) Refers to the inset street map on the pull-out map
(0) Located off the map

BEST OF
MALLORCA

Cala Mondragó: bay of dreams

BEST ☂

WHEN IT RAINS

ACTIVITIES TO BRIGHTEN YOUR DAY

FOR THE LOVE OF FILM

Passionate cinephiles make great company on a rainy evening. The *Cine Ciutat*, run by film fans as a cooperative, screens international movies in a range of original languages with subtitles.

➤ p. 51, In & Around Palma

LIFE IN THE SEVEN SEAS

Ever snuggled up to a stingray? With snorkelling opportunities, shark tanks and tanks where you can touch the fish, the *Palma Aquarium* makes for an exciting and interactive day out.

➤ p. 53, In & Around Palma

UNDERGROUND MALLORCA

Some of the island's most interesting charms are hidden beneath your feet in thousands of caves, of which five are accessible to the public. The *Coves de Campanet* are small but perfectly formed. They feature spaghetti-thin stalactites and stalagmites that are particularly impressive.

➤ p. 85, The North

FOREVER BLOWING BAUBLES

Vidrios de Arte Gordiola near Algaida is the oldest of the island's three glass-blowing workshops. Do as the Spanish royal family did and admire the workers' skill and the fragile beauty of what they create (photo).

➤ p. 128, The Centre

A SPIRITUAL JOURNEY THROUGH CHURCHES & CLOISTERS

The *Spiritual Mallorca* tour takes you to the religious heart of the island with the help of an affordable combined ticket – which includes the Convent de Francesc in Palma and the heavenly heights of the Cura monastery, and the popular pilgrimage site of Santuari de Lluc among others.

BEST 🐷

ON A BUDGET

FOR SMALLER WALLETS

A PALACE FOR EVERYONE
Come on in! Unlike most other palaces in Palma, the *Casal Solleric* opens its doors for visitors. Inside: a picture-perfect courtyard, an art gallery and a library.
➤ p. 44, In & Around Palma

AT HOME WITH JOAN MIRÓ
Of course, it's well worth paying the admission fee for the fantastic museum belonging to the *Fundació Pilar i Joan Miró* – which is housed in the artist's former home. However, on Saturday afternoons and certain other days you can also get in for free.
➤ p. 45, In & Around Palma

FREE CITY TOUR
Wander through Palma's old town taking in the main sites on a route from the Parc de la Mar via the main square (with its ancient olive tree) to the Plaça Espanya. *Mallorca Freetour* offers a great introduction to the island's

capital every day of the week except Sunday. There's no need to book; you can just show up.
➤ p. 50, In & Around Palma

INTO THE WILD
Fed up with all the crowds? Then head into the wild. *S'Albufera* nature park is home to many protected species. Take time for a wander through the wetlands here – they are free of asphalt, free of concrete, and free of charge (photo).
➤ p. 84, The North

ORGAN DONATED
An organist blows air through 25 pipes at the push of a key. Imagine how it must sound when it's played properly! You can pay a lot of money for concert tickets to find out; or, alternatively, you can attend one of the free rehearsals at the church of *Sant Andreu* in Santanyí.
➤ p. 114, The South

BEST

WITH CHILDREN

FUN FOR YOUNG & OLD

BOUNCE TO THE BEAT

Palma Jump, on the edge of the capital, has all manner of trampolines, climbing walls, tightropes and much much more. There are "bouncing parties" every Friday, which are popular with teenagers. DJs make sure the bopping is at least slightly rhythmical.
➤ p. 50, In & Around Palma

RELEASE YOUR INNER TARZAN

Vines, swings and rickety bridges strung between huge trees. *Jungle Parc Junior* in Bendinat offers adventures for kids aged four to eleven.
➤ p. 55 In & Around Palma

SCARY STUFF

Katmandu Park will keep kids entertained for hours. The House of Katmandu is a beautiful building in Tibetan style … which has been turned upside down and is full of scary surprises – watch out for the yeti.
➤ p. 60, The West

NEED AN ADRENALIN HIT?

If the Med's wavelets are too small and boring for you, then head to Port d'Alcúdia's *Hidropark*, where there are wave machines and slides galore (as well as chilled-out pools for little ones).
➤ p. 88, The North

FISHING FUN

You may need to get up at the crack of dawn but it is well worth it (even though it's your holiday) to accompany local fishermen as they go about their daily work. If you are really lucky you may see dolphins.
➤ p. 156, Good to know

COLLECTING FLOTSAM

A lot of stuff gets washed up on Mallorca's flat south coast – not only plastic, but also natural waste such as cuttlefish or seashells. Delve into your *Blue Peter* youth and create some holiday jewellery or home decorations.

BEST ⚑

CLASSIC EXPERIENCES

ONLY ON MALLORCA

THAT BIT CLOSER TO GOD …

Every village has its *ermita*, *monasteri* or *santuari*, mostly atop the summit of a nearby mountain. Some have been converted into lodgings with picnic spots. These are sacred places where locals meet to enjoy a barbecue with views of the island. One example is the *Ermita de la Trinitat*.
➤ p. 67, The West

GET SOME FRESH AIR

Late in the evening, Mallorcans *prendre la fresca*: sit outside their front doors to enjoy the cooler evening air and chat about the day. To soak up the atmosphere, visit the village squares of *Esporles* or *Bunyola* on any summer evening from 10pm onwards.
➤ p. 67 & 73, The West

RED EARTH & WHITE BLOSSOM

Magnificent pink-and-white blossoms against a backdrop of Mallorca's characteristic red soil. Experience a unique natural spectacle during the almond blossom season from late January to early March. In *Son Servera* it is even celebrated with a festival.
➤ p. 104, The East

SWEET TEMPTATION

You'll find the tastiest *ensaïmada* – a coiled bun made with lard and sprinkled with icing sugar – on Mallorca. To try one, head for the *Ca na Juanita* bakery in Alaró, which has been going for over 100 years (photo).
➤ p. 125, The Centre

FINGER-LICKING OILY BREAD

Mallorcans don't put butter on their bread. Instead, a Mallorca staple is *pa amb oli* (bread with olive oil), which can feature tomatoes, cheese, ham, olives, capers or marinated samphire. Perfect in its simplicity, the *Hostal d'Algaida* does a particularly good version.
➤ p. 128, The Centre

GET TO KNOW MALLORCA

Mallorca has multiple identities, from decadent partying in Palma to a solemn blessing in Muro

DISCOVER MALLORCA

Start your holiday with a stroll around the market in Santanyí

Picture the scene: a warm sunny evening, the sound of cicadas, the scent of pine trees and the backdrop of a picture-perfect bay with a white-sand beach – one of hundreds on the island. Holidays don't get much better than this.

SO VARIED & SO BEAUTIFUL

Mallorca is a magnet; the largest island in the Balearics attracts them all: kings, artists, pop stars, drop-outs and, most of all, tourists. Nowhere else in the Mediterranean is as varied or versatile, so it is little wonder that tourism is what drives the Mallorcan economy. Infamous as a holiday destination for the masses in the early years of cheap tourism, the island has developed into a multicultural microcosm with excellent infrastructure and some of the best-quality food around, without ruining its most important resource: overwhelming natural beauty.

Around 4000 BCE
The first cave dwellers settle Mallorca

123 BCE
Romans occupy Mallorca, founding both Pollentia and Palma

From CE 455
Vandal raids end Roman rule

From 903
Mallorca is conquered by Arabic Moors

1229
A victorious Jaume I, King of Aragon, enters Medina Mayurka (Palma) on 31 December

1276
Jaume II proclaims the Balearics as the Kingdom of

Visitors wanting to experience this aspect of the island will have to leave their hotel and strike out on their own: on foot, by bike or motorbike, by local bus, train or hire car. Mallorca's road network is exemplary; prices for hiring a car are no more expensive than elsewhere; and distances across the island don't exceed 90km.

SO MUCH TO SEE, SO LITTLE TIME

There is far too much to see on the 3,640km² island for a two-week holiday. In the north, there is the large double bay of Pollença-Alcúdia, tightly clasped between the two fingers of the Formentor and Isla de la Victoria peninsulas, plus the S'Albufera wetlands and the beautifully restored historic towns of Pollença, Alcúdia and Artà. In the east, the pretty hills of the Serra de Llevant are ideal for picturesque pottering, with countless small paths leading down to fjord-like bays, beautiful beaches and characterful ports. The south is hot and flat, and is characterised by beaches, dunes, pine groves and seawater lakes. Then there is the cherry on top of the island's cake: the wild west, including the imposing high mountains of the Serra de Tramuntana, which has more than 50 peaks over 1,000m, as well as bottomless gorges and steep rock faces – not forgetting one of the most exciting and stunning drives in Europe. The interior, *es Pla*, a high plateau occasionally interrupted by sleepy villages, is the bread basket and vegetable garden of the island. Last but not least is the capital, Palma, one of the most beautiful cities of the Mediterranean, which succeeds in preserving the old while creating something new in a process of constant reinvention. Palma effortlessly blends the

Mallorca; an era of flourishing trade begins

1814
After the end of Spain's Peninsular War against France, Mallorca is given its own liberal constitution

From 1960
Mass tourism starts in the Franco era

1983
The Balearic Islands become one of the 17 autonomous regions of democratic Spain

2016
The Ecotasa green tax is introduced

2021
Balearic Waste Law bans the use of some single-use plastics

island's 3,000-year history with trendy modern enterprises such as fashion boutiques, street-food stands and yoga retreats.

AND IS IT ECO-FRIENDLY? WELL ... IT'S GETTING THERE

Most summer visitors come for the sun, sand and sea and they aren't going to let themselves get distracted. Over 150 sandy beaches with a total length of some 50km are there to satisfy every wish. Thirty of the beaches are allowed to fly a Blue Flag, designating cleanliness. Environmental protection has become an increasingly important issue on the island ever since the environmental protection organisation GOB began exerting pressure on the island's government in the 1980s. The trend now is away from endless construction for tourist infrastructure and towards a more environmentally sound "soft tourism". Private and public initiatives have begun promoting sustainable development, and the local government has placed endangered habitats such as the S'Albufera wetlands and the Cala Mondragó under protected status. What's more, any construction in the Serra de Tramuntana, which constitutes a third of the island, is now subject to restrictions. In 2011, UNESCO added these mountains, with their vineyards, olive groves, almond orchards and citrus plantations to its list of World Heritage Sites.

FROM CANYONING & COASTEERING TO CULINARY CULTURE

If you're into active holidays, Mallorca is a perfect choice. Water-sports enthusiasts have over 40 marinas to choose from and a wealth of sailing, windsurfing and diving bases. Outdoor adventurers will find plenty of opportunities to climb, canyon and coasteer on the dramatic northern and western coasts. Both cyclists and motorcyclists love the winding mountain roads all over the island, and hikers just can't get enough of the fascinating interplay of mountains and sea. Over 6,000 restaurants, cafés and bars offer a broad range of culinary treats. From upmarket restaurants to newly trendy local hangouts and from chic beach bars to simple village pubs and cafés, there truly is something for everyone. And if you're here to party, check out the many happy hours in bars across the island.

STAY RELAXED

What do the Mallorcans have to say about the influx of tourists? Not much. Over the centuries, Mallorca has become accustomed to occupation and foreign influence by the Romans, Vandals, Arabs, Byzantines and by Spaniards from the mainland. Acceptance and integration have always been favoured over resistance by the islanders. For the visitor this *creates* a friendly atmosphere. When you visit Mallorca, remember that life here moves at a sedate pace. *Poc a poc*, "little by little", is the motto of the island – even during the busy season. So, if you find service slow in a restaurant or shop, resist the temptation to get impatient, and instead try soaking up a little bit of this *poc a poc* attitude yourself.

AT A GLANCE

869,000
Population

Leeds: 792,525

205
People aged over 100
Only 37 of these are men

3.5cm
The average length of a midwife toad, a species only found on Mallorca

3,640km^2
Surface area

Shropshire:
3,487km^2

HIGHEST MOUNTAIN: PUIG MAJOR

1,445m

LOWEST/HIGHEST SEA TEMPERATURE

13/27°C

IN FEB/AUG

HOURS OF SUN/YEAR

2,800

LONDON: ALMOST EXACTLY HALF AS MANY

PALMA
Largest city, with a population of 406,000

30g SAND PER DAY
the amount an average beachgoer takes with them when they head back to their accommodation in flip-flops, towels, swimming costume, etc. A total of 19 tons of sand is lost at Es Tren beach every year

THE LONGEST JETTY
Port Adriano for superyachts of up to 80m

BON PROFIT!
There are some 3,800 restaurants on the island

UNDERSTAND MALLORCA

NOBLE ADMIRER

Long before the first tourist invasion, the Austrian Archduke Ludwig Salvator (1847–1915), known as *Arxiduc* in Catalan, fell in love with the island's beauty – and with a number of the local beauties. And while his many illegitimate descendants do not bear his name, several roads and hiking trails are named after him. The Mallorcans still honour him today, because he made their island internationally famous, particularly among the Viennese nobility of the time – even the famous Empress Sisi of Austria was mad about Mallorca. Salvator (who is seen as the father of tourism to the Balearic Islands) eventually retired to his Son Marroig estate above the Sa Foradada Peninsula near Deià. His book, *The Balearic Islands in Words and Images*, remains an important resource for historians and researchers.

BALEARIC ISLANDS

Many Mallorcans have never visited their neighbouring islands, Menorca, Ibiza or Formentera, which form the Balearic Archipelago. Together these islands have nearly 1,500km of coastline and 370 beaches; the regional capital city is Palma. The establishment of the autonomous community of the Balearic Islands in 1983 did little to create a sense of shared identity, although this may be beginning to change.

BON DIA

Mallorca belongs to Spain, of course, but the local language is (since the 13th century) *Mallorquí*, a Catalan dialect. During Franco's regime (1939–1975), *Mallorquí* was banned, which explains why the locals love their language so much now. The linguistically (and to some extent politically) correct greeting here is, therefore, "bon dia" rather than "buenos días". Mallorcan Catalan is also the language of instruction and conversation at local schools and universities. In Palma, where the majority of immigrants live, the main language you'll hear on the streets is (Castilian) Spanish, or *Castellano*. It can be a bit confusing – many town and road signs are written in two languages: the official Mallorcan (e.g. Peguera, Ses Salines) and the old Spanish (Paguera, Las Salinas). But don't worry too much about it – you're on holiday, after all!

LIGHT & LIFE

Mallorca is green and bright throughout the year. The red earth, the white-pink almond blossom, which lasts from mid-January to March, and the ripe oranges in winter add extra splashes of colour to the green landscape. Some 1,500 types of plant are known on the island. Summer visitors love the bougainvillea's red-and-purple riot of colour and the pink oleanders lining entire streets. During the rainy winters, the underground cisterns fill up; oak, pine, almond, olive, carob, fig and lemon trees then draw water from them during the hot, dry summers. The millions of

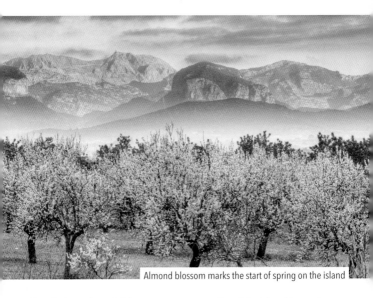

Almond blossom marks the start of spring on the island

pink-and-white almond blossoms in January are the first harbingers of spring. They are followed in March by yellow and white marguerites that cover meadows and arable fields. April brings wild purple gladioli; May brings fire-red poppies. After the first rainfall of autumn, yellow sorrel and wild orange marigolds liven up the scenery. Evergreen oak forests cover 150km² of the Serra de Tramuntana, and in the height of summer the extensive Aleppo pine forests resound with deafening cicada concerts.

The island may be rich in plant life, but there is no comparable abundance of animals. There are no larger mammals; what you will find are wild rabbits, field hares, martens, rats and mice as well as feral goats whose teeth wreak a lot of damage. The island's fauna is dominated by birds. Some almost extinct birds of prey have been reintroduced. Twitchers' hearts beat a little faster when they spot black vultures in the Tramuntana or even Eleonora's falcons and shearwaters on the cliffs around Dragonera and Cabrera.

INSIDER TIP
Vultures circling above you

CATALAN PHILOSOPHER

Tennis champion Rafael Nadal, Grand Prix motorcycle champion Jorge Lorenzo and artist Miquel Barceló are the island's most famous native sons. But will people still remember them 700 years from now? When it comes to Ramon Llull (1232–1315/16), there's no question. The works of this lay theologian, philosopher and missionary are still taught at universities around the world. If you want to follow in his footsteps on his native island, you need to head to the Randa hermitage,

Miramar near Valldemossa or the Franciscan monastery in Palma.

Llull lived during the Crusades and the Reconquista, when Spain was retaken by the Christians. In the 13th century, the majority of Spain's population was Muslim. This vocal, non-conformist thinker preached dialogue rather than violence and made multiple trips to North Africa to debate Muslim philosophers in Arabic. Many of his writings were in Catalan rather than Latin; he is consequently considered the founder of the written Catalan language. In that sense, he's a bit like the Catalan Shakespeare. He was also very productive, with over 265 works (mostly in Catalan) credited to him. This extensive oeuvre helped elevate Catalan to become a 'literary language'. Perhaps his most famous quote – 'Love makes servants of the free and gives slaves their freedom' – gives a sense of the open-minded nature of this great thinker.

HOME TIES

Culturally, the residents of the island feel closest to Catalonia. Their language isn't the only obvious sign: FC Barcelona also has an enormous fan following on Mallorca. However, many Mallorcans come from totally different regions of the country. There was a tourism and construction boom on the island from the 1960s to the 1980s, and many of its current residents came from Andalusia or Galicia to work as builders, waiters or cleaners. Another 20 per cent of the island's approximately 860,000 residents come from outside Spain, mostly from Morocco,

Ramon Llull memorial in Palma

Germany and the UK (around 16,000). There's very little friction within the island's diverse population; the Mallorcans are far too relaxed for that. Many have come and gone, they say, referring to the island's long history of settlement and colonisation.

ORGANIC WINE

Mallorca's wines are getting better and better. And these days, one-third of wine-growers on the island are using organic production methods. Spain's organic wine pioneer was Biel Majoral, who set up a small bodega *(canmajoral.com)* near Algaida in 1979. Jaume Mesquida in Porreres *(jaumemequida.com)* and Jaume de Puntiró in Santa Maria del Camí *(vinsjaumedepuntiro.com)* also produce sustainable wines. Many wine-growers are now planting native varieties of grapes again, including Manto Negro, Callet, Prensal Blanc and Malvasía de Banyalbufar. For further details, visit *bodegasmallorca.com*.

PIRATES ON THE HORIZON?

There's an expression on the island: *Ara que no hi ha pirates*. Translated literally, it means, "Now, as there are no pirates here," which means, "Now, while no one's looking." The expression reflects a long-standing historical reality for Mallorcans: pirate raids. The largest island in the western Mediterranean long served as an important port of trade, and Palma was home to wealthy merchants. But port cities like Pollença and Sóller also suffered raids by Barbary Corsairs from North Africa. Even today, the

TRUE OR FALSE?

AN END TO BEER O'CLOCK AND EGG AND CHIPS?

Mallorca is famous for being a home away from home for many Brits who want sun, sand and alcohol on holiday. The image we probably most associate with the island is of pasty-skinned Brits 'tanned' bright lobster red while ordering familiar food and cheap booze. However, there is a major campaign against this type of tourism on the part of the islanders and the local British consul. So, watch this space … In a few years Brits on Mallorca may be sipping small Spanish *cervezas* before tucking into *gambas* and talking to the people on the next table about the political crises in Spain and Britain.

A QUEUE-LOVING PEOPLE?

Mallorcans – like Brits – love a good queue and, just as in Britain, there is strict etiquette associated with waiting one's turn. The same studied patience is required in restaurants. On Mallorca, waiters will take their time to do things correctly. For example, when you come to pay, use the phrase *"me cobras, cuando puedas,"* which roughly translates as "when you have a moment, could you possibly bring the bill." This might be interpreted as slow service but it is just how things work here.

Hiking in the Serra de Tramuntana is an antidote to crowded beaches

Moros y Cristianos festivities in these places – where victorious battles against the invading forces are re-enacted – serve as a reminder of this history. The watchtowers that line Mallorca's coast also tell a story of constant trepidation. Some people even say that the rather tight-lipped nature of the island's residents is a result of this permanent threat; for their ancestors, the sea and the outside world were synonymous with danger.

SMUGGLERS' PATHS

Many of the hiking trails through the mountains and along the sea shore are paths that were used by smugglers well into the 20th century to transport sacks of cigarettes, alcohol and coffee (often from illegal speedboat drops) to their hideaways. These precious goods were then hawked by the criminal bosses at a great profit.

The greatest modern-day smuggler was Joan March who was born in 1880 to a family of pig farmers but who went on to become the richest man in Spain. Mallorca has his unscrupulous business sense to thank for its biggest and most beautiful *fincas*. March needed to unload his goods undetected, so he simply purchased large swathes of the coast to keep prying neighbours off his scent.

On S'Amador beach near Santanyí, a short, hidden path *(Itinerari de la punta de ses Gatoves)* leads you through the seaside scrub. If you see a spacious hole in the wall on the side of the road, you've found a *secret* (hiding spot). Goods from Barcelona were unloaded on the east coast near Artà, in places like Cala Estreta. In the

Tramuntana Mountains, the six-hour *Albarca–Cosconar–Puig Roig* hiking route passes through the smugglers' region, with jaw-dropping views of the Puig Roig mountain range.

TALAIOTS

Talaia means watchtower or lookout tower. The word *talaiot* comes from *talaia* and refers to the prehistoric megalithic structures found on Mallorca and the other Balearic islands. It is thought that these settlements, in existence from 1300 BCE up to the Roman occupation, served religious purposes. In most cases, the watchtower, up to 8m high and erected from extremely heavy blocks of stone, would have stood at the centre of the settlement. Mallorca boasts over 100 such prehistoric settlements.

MEDS FOR THE MED

Mallorca's sewage systems can have a hard time keeping up with demand, which sometimes leads to raw sewage being released into the sea. On top of this there are still no set rules limiting the number of boats allowed to anchor off Mallorca's coast or a rule banning them from releasing their sewage into the sea. And since many of the *puertos* on Mallorca do not have the facilities to cope with boats offloading their waste in port, many sailors have little option but to pollute the azure Mediterranean waters… However, there is a rule to protect the island's seaweed colonies. If a yacht or motorboat captain throws anchor into these protected areas, they can face fines of up to €2m. Neptune grass is

particularly worthy of protection as it helps maintain the biosphere underwater by cleaning the water and providing a playground for young fish.

FLYING STONES

For thousands of years, the indigenous people of Mallorca hunted animals and drove off intruders using *fones*, or slingshots. They were especially popular among the Roman legions for their accuracy. Today, Mallorcans are rediscovering the art of using these woven hemp slingshots in sport clubs, and the best slingers can win awards in competitions. The projectiles are usually stones, but children generally use tennis balls.

CHECK BEFORE YOU CHECK IN

Private letting of accommodation is a highly regulated business on Mallorca and regular checks are carried out by specialised inspectors who can issue fines of up to €400,000. The Tourism Law on which these rules depend was voted through by the Balearic parliament in 2017 and states that anyone letting out accommodation needs a licence and that all income derived from such letting has to be declared for tax purposes. The government has even set up an app, *Verificador alquiler turístico*, which can tell you if the place you are looking at provides legal accommodation. It is available on both iOS and Android. The island's council has set the number of guest beds on Mallorca at 430,000, of which 115,000 are in rented houses and flats.

INSIDER TIP
Rest easy

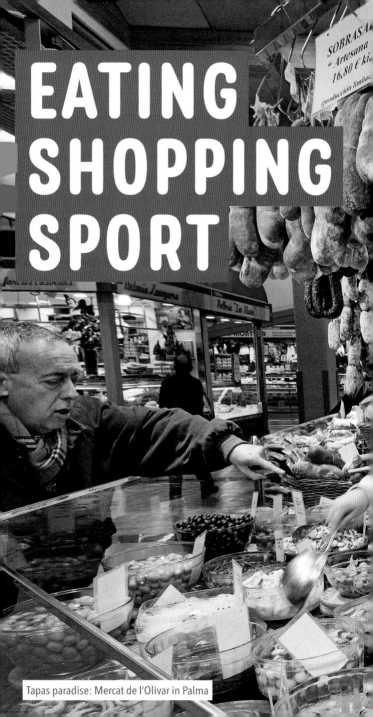

EATING
SHOPPING
SPORT

Tapas paradise: Mercat de l'Olivar in Palma

EATING & DRINKING

Mallorca is arguably the best holiday destination for foodies on the Med. The sheer number of restaurants acts as bait and their diversity – from small tapas bars, local dives and street-food stands to fine Michelin-starred cuisine – is enough to reel the gourmets in.

With over 3,800 restaurants on the island, you could go to a new one every night for ten years and still not have tasted everything! On top of what is already there, new places are opening all the time. The culinary landscape here is constantly shifting – and is all the better for it.

FUSION FOREVER

Fusion cooking is not a recent trend on Mallorca, but a reflection of its culinary history. Mallorca has always been a melting pot of diverse influences. Every wave of conquest and settlement has left its mark on the island's

cuisine. It may have begun with the Romans and Arabs but today it is northern Europeans who are ushering in the changes. The most traditional restaurants are the old-school *cellers*, rustic underground eateries where you can gorge on local delicacies surrounded by huge vats of wine while escaping the summer heat. More recently, young and exciting local chefs have emerged, determined to freshen up their island's basic peasant food and to give a new lease of life to dishes like roasted goat *(cabra al forn)* or *tumbet*, a classic baked veggie dish.

GASTRONOMIC ARCHAEOLOGY

Eating well has been a part of Mallorca's culture since time immemorial. And while the farmers and fishermen of centuries gone by ate simple fare, the feudal lords who ruled over them lived it up in their grand country estates and Palma palaces. In

Arròs brut, literally "dirty rice", is authentically Mallorcan and very tasty (right)

recent years, researchers have been investigating what these medieval Mallorcan millionaires ate. One chef involved in this "gastronomic archae-ology" is award-winning Tomeu Arbona. A full range of his foodie finds is available in his restaurant, *Fornet de la Soca* (see p. 48) in Palma.

SWEET PRAWNS, SPICY SALAMI

Mallorcan cooking depends on using the island's amazing fresh, local pro-duce. Black pigs and red sheep produce delicious meat and charcute-rie. Alongside this, there is fresh seafood, sun-ripened fruit and vegeta-bles (including outstanding oranges and almonds), the most virginal of olive oils and hand-harvested salt. It is every bit as delicious as it sounds. Seafood delicacies include salt-crusted fish and prawns from Sóller. The latter are almost sweet and are popular with gourmets. However, be careful when

ordering seafood dishes in restau-rants. The price is often not included and can come as a shock when you see it on the bill, so always check before you order.

Sobrassada is a hearty spreadable salami produced using *porc negre* (from the black pigs) and seasoned with spicy paprika. It is normally sold in different spice grades so be careful to get one at the level you want. The paprika does not just give it a distinc-tive flavour, it also helps preserve the meat. Meat eaters will also enjoy the island's tender roasted pork loins, lamb and rabbit. And for vegetarians, there is a wealth of mushroom and rice dishes.

Central ingredients to cooking here include paprika (obviously) but also fennel, parsley and garlic. *Allioli*, a gar-lic mayonnaise, is often served with meat. And there are – of course – onions with everything.

BREAD & PASTRIES

Bread with oil – *pa amb oli* – is one of Mallorca's best-loved dishes. To make it you toast (or ideally grill) a piece of bread, rub it with fresh garlic and then spread a puree using hard-skinned Ramallet tomatoes on it before adding the oil on top. A ham or cheese layer finishes it off perfectly before garnishing with olives or pickled samphire – a rich source of vitamin C.

Pastries can help satisfy your inter-meal hunger. Choose from *cocarroi* made with chard, and *empanades* made with meat, fish or vegetables. For pudding (some people even have it for breakfast), try *ensaïmada*, a lardy pastry normally baked in swirls and liberally dusted with icing sugar; plain or apricot varieties are available and some places even sell a version with *sobrassada*.

BON PROFIT!

Food has always played a big role on the island and it is not at all unusual for people to eat a three-course meal when they go out (at both lunch and dinner). As a result, prices are reasonable, particularly at lunch where nearly everywhere offers a *menú del día* – a good-value, fixed-price menu.

CHEERS!

Every good meal deserves a good wine and luckily there is a huge selection of local wines to choose from. In recent decades a group of innovative and passionate winemakers have turned Mallorca into something of a wine wonderland, producing a huge range of varieties, including *cava*. On Mallorca, it is normal to drink (a moderate amount) of wine at both lunch and at dinner. Most meals are accompanied by an open bottle and a carafe of water which is either fizzy *(amb/con gas)* or still *(sense/sin gas)*. Beer *(cervesa)* is growing in popularity partly thanks to some excellent local micro-breweries.

If you are into digestifs, give a local spirit *(chupito)* a try. The most traditional of them all is *hierbas*, with a base flavour of aniseed. Lots of families have their own secret *hierbas* recipe using different botanicals (everything from lemon verbena to camomile). There are sweet *(dulce)*, semi-dry *(mezclado)* and dry *(seca)* varieties. Try your *hierbas* on ice for an extra special taste sensation.

INSIDER TIP
A very cool herby shot

Vermouth is also enjoying a big renaissance on the island, with many local producers.

Round things off with an espresso *(café)* or a *cortado* (espresso with some milk). On Mallorca, people tend to only drink *café con leche*, milky coffee, for breakfast.

RESERVE EARLY

You are advised to book restaurant tables in advance. When you get to a restaurant, wait to be seated. After you have finished and have paid the bill, leave a tip on the small plate provided. The bill will usually include a *cubierto* (cover charge), plus a charge for bread and olives. IVA stands for VAT.

Today's Specials

Starters /Snacks

VARIAT
A Mallorcan mix of tapas: an interesting variety of small bites

TREMPÓ
A summer salad of tomatoes, onions and green peppers in olive oil

COCA
A Mallorcan take on pizza topped with red pepper or chard

SOPAS MALLORQUINES
A cabbage and pork stew served with sun-dried slices of bread *(sopas)*

Main Courses

TUMBET
Vegetable stew made from potato, aubergine and red pepper

FRIT MALLORQUÍ
Offal and vegetables laced with garlic and served with samphire

CONILL AMB CEBES
Rabbit and onions

LLOM AMB COL
Pork or pigeon wrapped in cabbage and braised in a wine broth with bacon, raisins and pine nuts

ARRÒS BRUT
A rice dish with three kinds of meat. The name means 'dirty rice' because the saffron colours the rice

Desserts

GATÓ D'AMETLLA AMB GELAT
A loose almond cake served with almond or vanilla ice cream

ENSAÏMADA
A pastry swirl covered in icing sugar

Drinks

HORCHATA D'AMETLLA
Almond milk

VI NEGRE
Red wine (typical Mallorcan grapes include Mantenegro and Callet)

VI BLANC
White wine (typical Mallorcan grapes include Prensal Blanc)

SHOPPING

POTTY FOR POTS

To cook like the islanders, you'll need traditional *greixoneras* and *olles*: brown clay pots that are standard in every Mallorcan kitchen. Pòrtol and Felanitx are known for their ceramics. Little bowls or plates in modern designs are perfect souvenirs; the potters will pack them carefully to ensure they won't break in transit. The ceramics fair *Fira de Fang* takes place in Marratxí in March.

ARTY PARTY

Nearly 3,000 painters are said to live and work on Mallorca. The most famous is Miquel Barceló but Bernardí Roig, Susy Gómez, and Guillem Nadal are also internationally successful. The galleries *Pelaires* (see p. 50), *Fran Reus (Passeig de Mallorca 4)* and *Frank Krüger (C/ Costa d'en Brossa 3)* in Palma regularly exhibit surprising works by local artists at varying prices.

You can get the best overview of local art during the *Nit de l'Art* gallery night on the third weekend of September in Palma.

TASTY SOUVENIRS

Take something delicious home to remind you of Mallorca. The incomparable *ensaimadas* are pastry swirls sold with or without filling. In supermarkets you will find *hierbas*, the bright green herbal aniseed liqueur.

Delicious *Mel de na Marta* comes from Artà. Marta sells her honey – mainly from live oak and carob blossoms – at the weekly markets in Pollença *(Sun)*, Artà *(Tue)*, and Sineu *(Wed)*, as well as in organic food shops. Cold-pressed olive oil of the best quality is available in lots of shops as are the salt flakes (Flor de Sal) harvested in the Es Trenc saltworks. There are good-quality

INSIDER TIP
Sweet gold

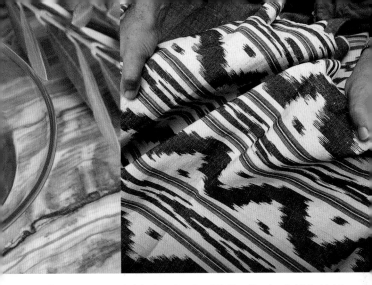

Mallorcan souvenirs include high-quality olive oil (left) and handmade fabrics (right)

markets with all these delicacies across the island during harvest season.

LEATHER & LINEN

Inca, its neighbouring villages and Llucmajor are at the heart of a leather industry that is once again flourishing. It is worth looking out for shoes as they are relatively cheap to buy. The simplest shoe available is the *aubarca*, a comfortable and good-value sandal that originates from Menorca. The most authentic ones are those using car tyres as soles, but fancier versions featuring high heels and glitter are available too.

Traditional decorative fabrics, known as *ikats*, with a distinctive Malaysian-style tongue pattern are still woven in Santa Maria and in Pollença. The heavy, natural linen fabrics *(robes de llengo)* are labour-intensive to produce, hence not that cheap. You can buy them by the metre, or in sets, as cushion covers and blankets.

MEMORIES THAT GLISTEN

Tired of faux pearls? Ignore the enormous shops around Manacor and scour the weekly markets for real Mallorcan artisanal handicrafts and unique jewellery. Recommended markets include Alcúdia *(Tue)*, Santanyí *(Wed)* and Campos.

ALMOND FLOWERS AT HOME

Thanks to its floral bouquet, the almond perfume "Flor d'Ametler Classic" is the perfect way to take some of the island's scent back home. It is the essence of the island, produced using an ancient family recipe. What makes it even more special is that all the bottles (they come in 30ml and 50ml sizes) come with a hand-picked almond flower.

SPORT & ACTIVITIES

When the thermometer hits the 40-degree mark, many holiday-makers feel the only way to go is down to the sea. It's no wonder water sports such as swimming, diving, sailing and windsurfing are much in demand. But the Mediterranean climate provides ideal conditions for active sport holidays all year round, be it on your bike or on a hiking trip through the mountains.

CANYONING

Canyoning is one of Mallorca's best-kept secrets. Commercial tour operators such as *Món d'Aventura (prices from 50 euros | tel. 9 71 53 52 48 | mondaventura.com)* and *Experience Mallorca (tel. 6 87 35 89 22 | experience-mallorca. com)* lead groups through the mountains on the west and north coast that are up to 1,500m high and criss-crossed by many small streams. These mountain streams, called *torrents* or *barrancs*, have carved deep grooves into the calciferous rocks, creating great climbing routes for people of all abilities. In the winter, the gorges are often full of water, cascades and churn-holes. In the summer, they are dry and cool. Since most of the time you climb from the top down, children don't need that much strength, but they need to be dexterous and up for an adventure. They are roped up all the time and are accompanied by experienced climbers. A helmet is mandatory. All gear is provided, including wetsuits in winter.

COASTEERING

Simply the best outdoor activity in summer. Roped up, with a helmet and a guide, you climb along the steep cliffs on the coast. Don't worry, there's little risk of injury. If you miss a grip,

Sailing around the island's 554-km coast is a popular maritime activity

you just take a refreshing plunge into the sea beneath you. Still, you should have a head for heights and enjoy sports. *Món d'Aventura (prices from 40 euros | tel. 9 71 53 52 48 | mondaventura.com)* and *Escull Aventura (prices from 60 euros | tel. 6 91 23 02 91 | escullaventura.com)* offer half-day tours; both are based in Pollença.

CYCLING

In spring and autumn, hobby and professional cyclists can be found on the island in their thousands. In a bid to promote sustainable tourism in the off seasons, the island government constantly extends the network of cycle paths and is working on an app showing suitable routes. Those wanting to take it easy are best off in the flat area between Campanet and Campos, while any aspiring pros should head to the mountain passes in the Tramuntana. The island's greatest cycling challenge is up here – the Coll de Puig Major. At an altitude of nearly 1,000m, there are no higher climbs on Mallorca. The switchback road above the bay of Sa Calobra is another pretty serious challenge.

Bikes of all kinds can be hired in every resort from around 10 euros per day. Find good cycling routes on *cycling-friendly.com*.

DIVING

Mallorca's underwater world is especially interesting along the rocky parts of the coast and off the Dragonera and Cabrera archipelagos. The water is clearest between April and June. There are diving schools all over the island. A PADI beginner's certificate *(Scuba Diver)* takes two to three days. Prices start at around 280 euros. To book onto an organised dive, prices start at 56 euros.

Beach rides and guided hacks are a great way to explore

INSIDER TIP
Underwater with a buddy

For this you get all the equipment and a buddy. One of the best spots is the area off the beautiful coastal village of Sant Elm where the *Scuba Activa* diving school is based *(tel. 9 71 23 91 02 | scuba-activa.com)*.

In Calvià, you can dive without a certificate: *Peter Diving (C/ Punta Negra 12 | tel. 9 71 75 20 26 | 2 hrs total with at least 40 mins diving from 65 euros | C/ Punta Negra 12 | Tel. 9 71 75 20 26 | peterdiving.com)* offers a mixed day of snorkelling and scuba diving. As the oxygen tank floats on the surface of the water you can dive right in without needing your PADI (they do a comprehensive safety briefing).

GOLF

Boasting 24 playable courses, Mallorca has turned itself into a new European golfing mecca these days. Save a lot on money on your golfing holiday with the *Mallorca Golfcard* for 119 euros *(mallorca-golfcard.com)*.

HIKING

Hiking on Mallorca is first and foremost possible on the long-distance GR-221 trail which leads through the Tramuntana mountains on the west coast in several segments. The *Ruta de Pedra en Sec (Drywall Trail)* runs for more than 150km between Andratx and Port de Pollença. It leads through an ancient cultivated landscape with terraced fields and mountain farms, oaks, pines and wild olive trees. The sea view is what makes this hiking experience unforgettable. You can find accommodation in eight *refugis* (mountain huts, seven of which offer half board) in Esporles, Deià, Sóller, Alaró, Lloseta, Escorca and Pollença *(overnight stay from 14 euros, breakfast from around 5.50 euros)*. Be sure to book early at short.travel/mlc13.

The island's local government has recently put together 14 👪 family-friendly, short, circular walks, for which you can find English-speaking maps in all tourist information offices. If you are out hiking, you will not be able to miss the unmistakable smell of wild rosemary. Close your eyes, drink it in – and commit to memory the heady aroma of a Mallorcan summer.

HORSE RIDING

There are *Ranchos* or *Clubs Hípic* in nearly every resort. As the island is almost entirely in private hands and has many fences, it is best to join a guided hack. *Son Menut* horse riding centre *(Camí de Son Negre | www. sonmenut.com | day hack 110 euros including water and a light lunch, 1 hr 25 euros | Camí de Son Negre | exit the Ma5120 at km 75 | Tel. 9 71 58 29 20 | sonmenut.com)* in Felanitx hires out Andalusian stallions to experienced riders. At the finca-turned-sports-hotel *Predio Son Serra* in Can Picafort *(guided hack 1 hr. 33 euros, ten rides 300 euros | Tel. 9 71 53 79 80 | finca-son-serra.com)* classes and long stays are the focus of attention.

KITESURFING & WINDSURFING

On Mallorca, kitesurfing is only allowed in the bay of Pollença where you will find the *Kite Mallorca* school *(3-day course with 10 hrs total surfing 300 euros | tel. 6 47 89 11 22 | kitemallorca.com)*.

Windsurfers get their money's worth in the broad bays of Alcúdia, Son Serra de Marina or Sa Rápita. Courses are offered by: *Wind & Friends Watersports* (see p. 88) in Alcúdia, or *Mallorca Adventure Sports (2 hrs 50 euros | tel. 6 29 47 22 68 | www. mallorcaadventuresports.com)* in Pollença, Portals Nous and Can Pastilla, among others.

SAILING

There are 41 marinas along Mallorca's 550km long and varied coastline where you can book courses, pass your captain's exam or charter a boat, e.g. at *Charter del Mar (1 week from 1,550 euros | tel. 6 06 59 17 84 | charterdelmar.com)* in Palma, or *CM Charter Mallorca (1 week from 2,450 euros | tel. 9 71 86 73 32 | www. cmcharter.de)* in Pollença.

STAND-UP PADDLEBOARDING

Glide regally over the water. Stand-up paddleboarding (SUP) is the very much the 'in' water sport on Mallorca at the moment. Boards can be rented near virtually every body of water *(from 10 euros an hour)*. There are also beginners' courses on offer in many places. There is no better way to experience the natural world and get some exercise.

REGIONAL OVERVIEW

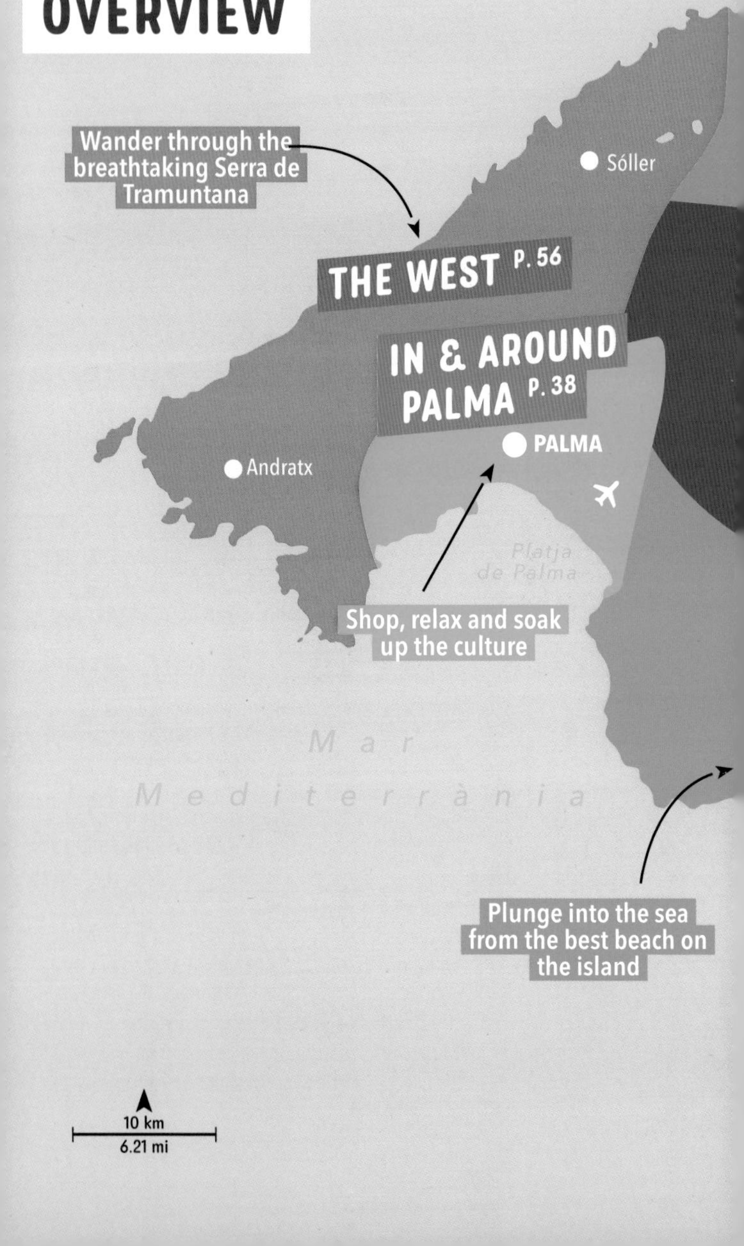

Wander through the breathtaking Serra de Tramuntana

● Sóller

THE WEST P. 56

IN & AROUND PALMA P. 38

● Andratx

● PALMA

✈

Platja de Palma

Shop, relax and soak up the culture

Mar Mediterrània

Plunge into the sea from the best beach on the island

▲
10 km
6.21 mi

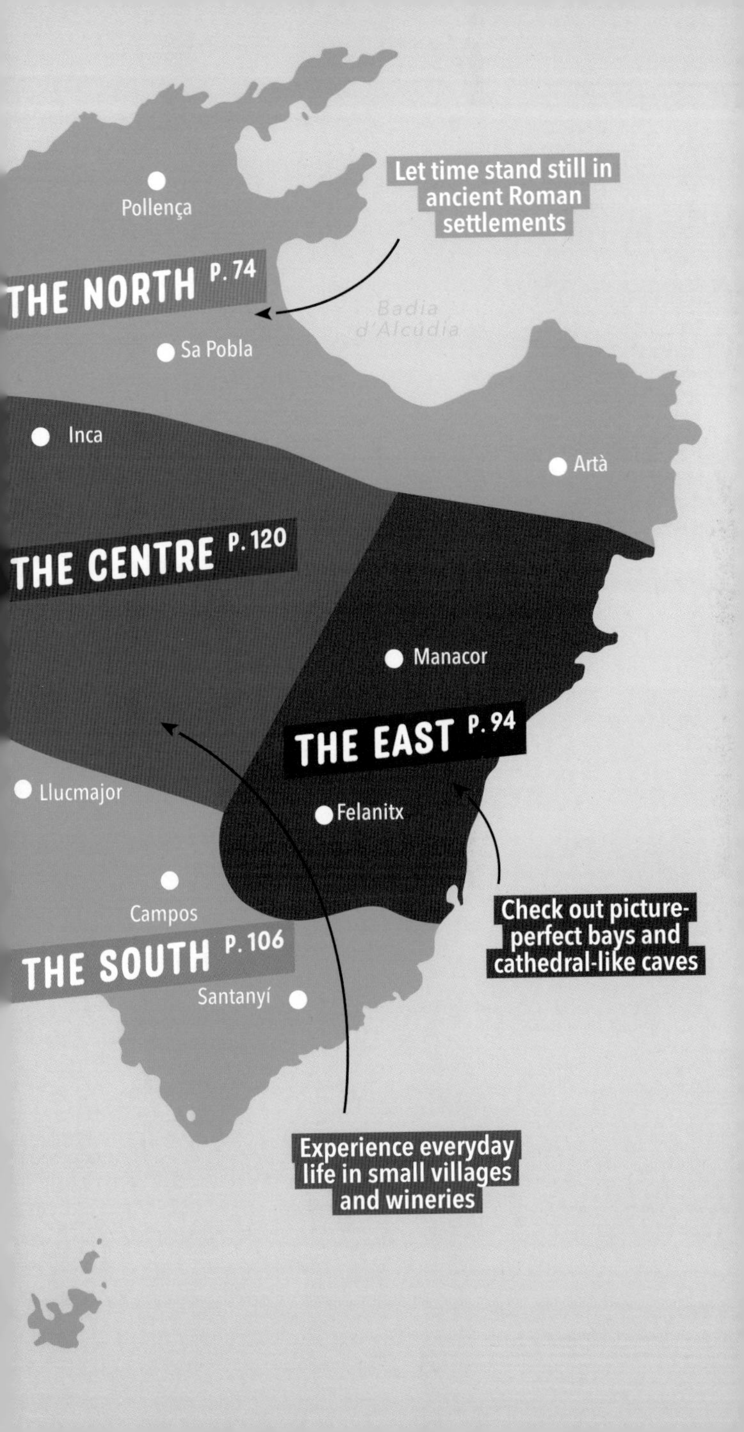

Pollença

Let time stand still in ancient Roman settlements

THE NORTH P. 74

Badia d'Alcúdia

Sa Pobla

Inca

Artà

THE CENTRE P. 120

Manacor

THE EAST P. 94

Llucmajor

Felanitx

Check out picture-perfect bays and cathedral-like caves

Campos

THE SOUTH P. 106

Santanyí

Experience everyday life in small villages and wineries

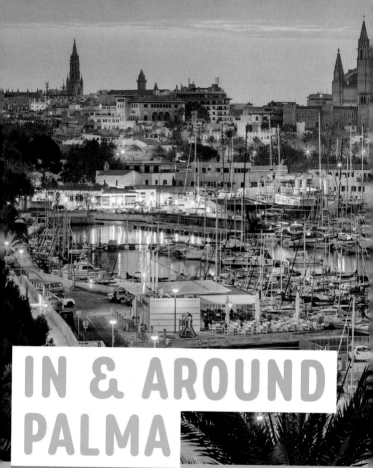

IN & AROUND PALMA

SIMPLY IRRESISTIBLE

One of the most beautiful cities on the Mediterranean, Palma is undoubtedly where most of the island's action takes place. Almost half of the island's residents – about 407,000 people – live in this pulsating city and its adjoining districts.

The best way to enjoy the city's ambience is, first of all, to leave your car in one of the blue parking zones (see p. 154) as driving and parking in many of the narrow, one-way streets in the centre is only open to residents. Then you can set off and stroll through one of the

Even from the harbour, Palma's mighty cathedral can't be ignored

largest preserved medieval cities on the Mediterranean. Discover the peaceful inner courtyards of sumptuous noblemen's palaces and the wealth of buzzing cafés, which fill the centre. There are also dark, incense-scented churches which sit right next to the bright lights of the market halls. Finally, the beautiful, spacious *plaças* bordered by shady arcades are perfect for relaxing after seeing the sights

The double-decker buses on the number 50 route stop at all the tourist attractions. For 12 euros you can hop on and off all day.

IN & AROUND PALMA

Ma-20

Carrer de Sevilla

Carrer d'Albó

A. de Picasso

Carrer de

Carrer d'Alzina

Carrer de Triana

Carrer del Vinyet

Carrer del Parc

Carrer de Soló

Camí dels Reis

Camí de Génova

Carrer d'Andrea Doria

Carrer de les Illes Balears

Camí dels Reis

Ma-20

Carrer de Son Armadans

Avinguda de Gabr

Port
de Palma

Tito's

Carrer del Dos de Maig

Carrer de la Salut

Avinguda de Joan Miró

Mercat
1930

10 Castell de Bellver

Carrer de Francesc Vidal Sureda

Ma-1

12 Fundació Pilar i Joan Miró ★

9 Port de Portals ★

A. de Joan Miró

11 Jardins de
Marivent

Avinguda de Gabriel Roca

Moll de Ponent

Moll de Paraires

Porto Pí

▲
500 m
547 yd

Cine Ciutat

Mercado Gastronómico San Juan

Maraca Club

Carrer del General Riera

Carrer de Ticià

A. Gaspar Bennàsar

Carrer de la Reina Maria Cristina

Carrer d'Eusebi Estada

Carrer de Jacint Verdaguer

Carrer d'Aragó

Carrer de Jesús

Carrer de Goethe

Sibilla

Carrer Isidoro Antillón

La Rambla

Sa Formatgeria

Akzent

Cafès Llofriu

Passeig Mallorca

Fornet de la Soca

Marc Fosh

Especias Crespi

Carrer de Lluís Martí

Can Balaguer

Can Miquel

Fera

Gran Hotel ★

Carrer de Manacor

Blue Jazz Club & Sky Bar

Casal Solleric

La Rosa Vermuteria

Mimbreria Vidal

Es Baluard ★

13 %

Estanc d'es Born

Colmado Santo Domingo

Avinguda de Gabriel Alomar

Carrer de Joan Alcover

Kaelum Club

Can Eduardo

Jazz Voyeur Club

La Bodeguita del Medio

Palau March Museu

Convent de Sant Francesc

La Seu – Palma cathedral ★

Museu de Mallorca

Banys Arabs

Palau de S'Almudaina

Carrer de Joan Maragall

Avinguda Adolfo Suárez

Es Mollet

Platja de Palma

MARCO POLO HIGHLIGHTS

★ **LA SEU – PALMA CATHEDRAL**
The most beautiful combination of light and stone anywhere in the Mediterranean ➤ p. 42

★ **ES BALUARD**
Modern art in a former fortress with great views over the city ➤ p. 44

★ **FUNDACIÓ PILAR I JOAN MIRÓ**
Memorial and museum in the former home of the artist ➤ p.45

★ **GRAN HOTEL**
The most striking example of the city's restored art nouveau architecture ➤ p. 45

★ **PORT DE PORTALS**
A mini-Marbella, perfect for posing and people-watching ➤ p. 55

PALMA

(□ E/F7) **You can explore Palma more economically and away from the main tourist routes by taking the municipal buses. Bus number 2 covers the city centre, while the number 7 runs from the villas in Son Vida to the run-down district of Son Gotleu** *(single 1.50 euros | emtpalma.es).*

WHERE TO START?

□ c6 Start your walking tour at **La Seu**, then cross through the upper old town via Plaça Major, Plaça Espanya, the historic quarter and Plaça Llotja to the port. Parking: the car park on Parc de la Mar directly below the cathedral is well placed. Alternatively, park further out and take the city bus EMT *(Line 15)* to Plaça de la Reina.

SIGHTSEEING

1 PALAU DE S'ALMUDAINA

Seen from the sea, the cathedral and the royal palace appear to be one and the same building. The former Alcázar of the Emir and later a residence of the kings of Aragon, today the palace houses the island's military headquarters and accommodates King Felipe VI when he spends time on Mallorca. The highlights of the palace are the royal chambers and the Gothic chapel of Santa Ana. *Tue–Sun April–Sept 10am–7pm, Oct–March 10am–5pm |* admission 7 euros | Wed and Thu summer 5–7pm, winter 3–5pm free for EU citizens (bring an ID card/passport) | C/ Palau Reial s/n | ⊙ 1.5 hrs | □ c5–6

2 LA SEU – PALMA CATHEDRAL ★

The most famous building on the island sits resplendently high up above the sea. The main nave, some 110m long, boasts 14 slim pillars, just under 22m high and the large rose window in the main apse (11.5m in diameter with a total area of around 100m²) is made up of 1,200 pieces of glass. When light bursts through it from outside, it transforms the rays of the sun into a kaleidoscope-like explosion of colour. This effect is particularly magical on 2 February and 11 November each year, when the reflection of the rose window on the eastern façade lines up to sit perfectly below the window on the western side.

Another enchanting sight is the Gaudí chandelier above the altar – and the *Feeding of the 5,000* in St Peter's Chapel, a giant ceramic work by the Mallorcan artist Miquel Barceló. From May to October, visitors are now able to explore the roof from where there are breathtaking views over the city and the sea *(admission 12 euros, sign up on the website). Mon–Fri June–Sept 10am–6.15pm, April/May and Oct 10am–5.15pm, Nov–March 10am–3.15pm, Sat all year round 10am–2.15pm | admission 7 euros Plaça Almoina | catedraldemallorca. info | ⊙ 1 hr, 2 hrs with roof tour |* □ c6

INSIDER TIP
215 steps up in the air

▣ BANYS ARABS

Arabic baths – but all that is left to see is a dome and pillars with various 10th-century capitals. However, the gardens are a good spot for relaxing. The gardens and baths belong to the *Font i Roig* palace, to which they are connected by a bridge. *Daily 9am–7pm | admission 2.50 euros | C/ de Serra 7 | ⏱ 45 mins | ▥ d6*

▣ MUSEU DE MALLORCA

During the 13th century, Mallorca became a major centre in the Western Mediterranean. At the Museu de Mallorca you will learn what this meant for the lives of the islanders. The museum has over 400 artefacts from eight centuries of the island's history. *Tue–Fri 10am–6pm, Sat/Sun 11am–2pm | admission 2.40 euros | C/ Sa Portella 5 | ⏱ 1.t hrs | ▥ d6*

▣ CONVENT DE SANT FRANCESC

The highlights of the otherwise fairly sober church façade are the rose window and the Baroque portal. Inside the large 17th-century basilica, there is a magnificent Baroque altar and the tomb of philosopher and missionary Ramón Llull. The monastery building with its beautiful Gothic cloisters houses a school. *Mon–Sat 10am–1pm and 2–6pm | admission 5 euros | Plaça Sant Francesc 7 | ⏱ 1 hr | ▥ e5*

▣ PALAU MARCH MUSEU ☂

In 2003, the descendants of legendary banker Joan March opened their city palace to the public to display an impressive art collection, among it a Neapolitan nativity scene with over 1,000 pieces. The ground floor houses a pretty branch of the Cappuccino chain of coffee shops. *Mon–Fri*

Stained glass windows create magical lighting effects inside La Seu

Can Rei's mosaic-covered façade

as the stunningly beautiful 🐟 *Can Balaguer (Tue–Sat 10am–7pm, Sun 10am–3pm | C/ Unió 3 | canbalaguer. palma.cat | free admission | ⊙ 45 mins | ⊞ c4).* Even back in the 19th century, Archduke Ludwig Salvador considered it one of the most important buildings in Palma. Also free and easy to visit is 🐟 *Casal Solleric (Tue–Sat 11am–2pm and 3.30–8.30pm, Sun 11am–2.30pm | Passeig des Born 27 | casalsolleric. palma.cat | ⊙ 1 hr | ⊞ b4).* which has been converted into a gallery and café.

In the week around Corpus Christi (May/ June) around a third of the 154 city palaces open their doors – and their *patios* – to the public. Some even hold concerts *(more information in all tourist offices).*

INSIDER TIP
A look behind the scenes

April–Oct 10am–6.30pm, Nov–March 10am–5pm, Sat all year round 10am–2pm | admission 4.50 euros | C/ Palau Reial 18 | fundacionbmarch.es | ⊙ 1 hr | ⊞ c5

🔢 CAN BALAGUER & CASAL SOLLERIC PALACES

Around the cathedral in the old city, there are a large number of *palaus* ("palaces") that were once the homes of rich merchants or Mallorca's nobility. Most were built in the 15th and 16th centuries in an Italianate style. Their street-facing façades look almost like fortresses, but inside their *patios* (courtyards) are delicately decorated with flowers. Only a few of these internal areas are open to the public, such

🔢 ES BALUARD ★

This modern building fits in brilliantly with Palma's historic fortifications, forming a fascinating contrast to the contemporary Spanish and international artworks it houses. There are great views of the port and cathedral from the roof terraces. *Tue–Sat 10am–8pm, Sun 10am–3pm | admission 6 euros, free on public holidays | Plaça Porta de Santa Catalina 10 | esbaluard.org | ⊙ 1.5 hrs | ⊞ 14*

🔢 PORT

Just below the cathedral, a long jetty extends out into the sea and marks the edge of the port. This is also where the ships leave for the one-hour *Cruceros Marco Polo* cruises around the harbour *(www.crucerosmarcopolo.*

com | March–Oct Mon–Sat hourly 11am–4pm | 12 euros/pers | cruceros marcopolo.com); a refreshing and relaxing change for visitors whose feet need a break. *a–b 5–6*

🔟 CASTELL DE BELLVER

Sturdy and massive from the outside while rather elegant in its circular loggia-lined interior courtyard, the royal castle dominates the town. Begun under Jaume I and completed in 1309, it served only briefly as a residence for Jaume II, before becoming a dungeon and a place of terrible pogroms against the Jewish population (14th century). Today, the castle houses the city's historical museum while the courtyard is used for concerts. The view of the city and port alone makes the drive up worthwhile. *Tue–Sat April–Sept 8.30am–7pm, Oct–March 10am–6pm, Sun all year round 10am–3pm | admission 4 euros, Sun free | ⏱ 45 mins | E7*

🔟 JARDINS DE MARIVENT 🐛

Want to see some of Miró's art? Then spend time wondering around the garden of the Spanish royal family's Mallorcan summer residence. The majestic Jardins de Marivent are home to 12 Miró bronze sculptures and a visit won't cost you a thing. When Felipe VI and his family are on the island (for example at Easter), the gardens' gates are sadly closed. *Daily May–Sept 9am–8pm, Oct–April 9am–4.30pm | Av. de Joan Miró 229 | Cala Major | ⏱ 30 mins | E8*

INSIDER TIP
Royal gardens

🔟 FUNDACIÓ PILAR I JOAN MIRÓ ⭐

If the Jardins de Marivent have not scratched your Miró itch … Following the wishes of Joan Miró (1893–1983), a Catalan by birth who made Mallorca his home, the artist's studio and residence were converted into a "place where people live, create and talk together". Part of Miró's artistic estate can be seen in the beautiful museum building designed by Rafael Moneo (it also regularly houses changing exhibitions). Don't miss the park and the café with a wall mosaic. At certain times, Miró's studio is also open to visitors. *Tue–Sat mid-May–mid-Sept 10am–7pm, mid-Sept–mid-May 10am–6pm, Sun all year round 10am–3pm | 🐛 admission 7.50 euros, free on Sat from 3pm and on first Sun in the month as well as open days | C/ Saridakis 29 | Cala Major | miro.palma demallorca.es | ⏱ 1.5 hrs | E8*

ART NOUVEAU BUILDINGS

In Palma some beautifully restored façades display the Catalan version of Art Nouveau, *Modernisme*. The *Edifici Casayas* on Plaça Mercat, was built between 1908 and 1911 by Francesc Roca. Diagonally opposite, arguably the city's most beautiful Art Nouveau façade looks down on the Plaça Weyler: the ⭐ *Gran Hotel (Mon–Sat 10am–8pm, Sun 11am–2pm | admission 4 euros | d4)* was built in 1901–03 by Lluís Domenec i Montaner and today houses an art gallery with restaurant. Standing next to each other on the Plaça Marqués de Palmer, the houses *Can Rei* and *L'Aguila* were built between 1908 and 1909 and are famous for their colourful mosaics. It is here that the influence of the great master of Catalan *Modernisme*, Antoni Gaudí, is most visible. In contrast, *Can Corbella*, in Carrer Jaume II, shows Moorish influence.

PLAÇAS (SQUARES)

Find a place to sit and order a cup of coffee or a glass of wine before watching the world go by: this is the favourite pastime of locals and visitors alike on Palma's squares. The *Plaça de Cort* (⬚ d5) is a pedestrianised town hall square with an olive tree that has been standing in front of the *ajuntament* for several hundred years. The stock-exchange square, *Plaça Llotja* (⬚ b5), has views of the 15th-century former maritime stock exchange and the port. The rectangular and pretty *Plaça Major* (⬚ d4), the main square in the upper town, is framed by the yellow façades of houses and arcades, and is often overrun by tourists.

At the *Plaça Espanya* (⬚ e2), Jaume I looks down from his pedestal through a swarm of pigeons onto this busy transport hub with the bus station and terminus of the Sóller railway. Round the corner, shoppers and foodies meet at *Plaça de l'Olivar* (⬚ e3), before or after visiting the *Mercat d'Olivar*, the city's largest covered market and home to *Cervecería Anfos (first floor of the market | tel. 9 71 72 91 20)* where Trini and Manolo will put your fresh market purchases straight on the grill.

INSIDER TIP
Hot off the grill

The square where everybody ends up at one stage or another is the *Plaça Rei Joan Carles* (⬚ b-c4), with the turtle obelisk in its centre. Both the *Bar Bosch* and *Café Solleric* are normally full to bursting.

EATING & DRINKING

Starting at 8pm, the entire district of *Santa Catalina* is transformed into an open-air buffet with international offerings. There are many restaurants to choose from in the traffic-free *Carrer Fábrica* whose pavements are always packed with tables. Top tips are *Duke (Mon–Sat 1–4pm and 7.30–11pm | C/ Soler 36 | tel. 9 71 07 17 38 | dukepalma.com | €€)* which serves light fresh food, and *Nuru (Mon–Sat 1–3.30pm and 7–11pm | C/ Anníbal 11 | tel. 8 71 96 49 31 | nuru.restaurant | €€)* which specialises in Asian fusion cooking. *Simply Delicious (Mon–Sat 11am–5pm | Plaça Navegació 5 | tel. 6 00 67 37 22 | simplydelicious.es | €€)* serves Middle Eastern food and is (perhaps surprisingly) every bit as good as its name suggests.

If you're after excellent homely food, take a seat at the bar of *Joan Frau (Mon–Sat 7am–5pm | Plaça de la Navegació | mercatdesantacatalina.com | €)* in the Mercat de Santa Catalina covered market. She has been serving typical Mallorcan tapas for over 50 years; try the stuffed aubergines and *Coca de Verdura*, a veggie pizza-like dish. If you're lucky, you may be given a table *behind* the bar!

INSIDER TIP
The best tables in the house

The impressive olive tree on Plaça de Cort is several hundred years old

13 %

This lower ground-floor eatery offers good food and good value in the posh Carrer Feliu. Fresh colours dominate the décor while the small Mediterranean dishes are tasty. They have a carefully curated wine list from which you can order by the glass. *Mon–Sat from 12.30pm | C/ Feliu 13 | a side street of Passeig des Born | 13por ciento.com | closed Sun | €–€€ | ▥ b4*

CAN EDUARDO

One of the best seafood restaurants in town (the mussels are particularly good). Sitting right next to the fish market (Sa Llotja des Peix), you won't get fresher fish anywhere. *Daily from 1pm, closed Nov–Feb and Sun after-noons | C/ Contramuelle | Es Mollet | tel. 9 71 72 11 82 | caneduardo.com | €€ | ▥ a5*

CAN MIQUEL

This well-established ice-cream parlour offers a large selection of divine flavours at its two stores at *Carrer Montcades 9* and *Av. Jaume III 6*. In winter, the foodie fun carries on with pastries and chocolates and hot drinks – all made in house, of course. *Daily from 8.30am | FB: canmiquel1979 | ▥ b4*

ES MOLLET

A gifted chef magics up wonderful grilled fish, to be enjoyed with views over the small port of Es Molinar/Portixol in the east of Palma. However, the prices may bring you back to earth. *Tue–Sat 1–4pm and 7.30–11.30pm | C/ Sirena 1 | tel. 9 71 24 71 09 | €€€ | ▥ F7*

FERA

Just off the busy shopping street of *Jaume III*, Austrian chef Simon

Petutshnig serves up Mediterranean-Asian fusion food so good you will need time to savour it. The setting in a restored palace and the carefully selected wines aren't bad either. At lunchtime the set menu is a bargain. There are also veggie and vegan menus. Not hungry? You are welcome to just have a drink at the bar. *Daily from 1pm | C/ de la Concepció 4 | tel. 9 71 59 53 01 | ferapalma.com | €€–€€€ | b4*

FORNET DE LA SOCA

The award-winning chef Tomeu Arbona has taken over *Forn des Teatre*, the old bakery in this stylish Art Nouveau building and now serves his own delicious bread and pastries here. *Tue–Sun 7.30am–8pm | Plaça de Weyler 9 | d4*

MARC FOSH

Michelin-starred chef Marc Fosh and his team create stunning dishes using seasonal produce in this bright and sunny restaurant (it has its own patio too) in the *Convent de la Missió* hotel. *Daily 1–3pm and 7.30–10pm | C/ Missió 7a | tel. 9 71 72 01 14 | marc fosh.com | €€–€€€ | d3*

MERCADO GASTRONÓMICO SAN JUAN

The market in the former slaughter-house S'Escorxador has blossomed into the city's best area to eat tapas. You can choose from 16 stalls. The ambience is very Spanish and the place is packed at the weekend. *Daily 12:30pm–midnight, Thu–Sat later | C/ de l'Emperadriu Eugènia 6 | mercado sanjuanpalma.es | € | F7*

MERCAT 1930

If you want to do a tapas crawl, the Mercat 1930 on Palma's seafront is great. *Daily 12pm–midnight, Fri/Sat later | Av. Gabriel Roca 33 | mercat1930. com | €–€€ | E7*

SIBILLA

Should you be overcome by hunger while out shopping on the pedestrianised promenade of Blanquerna, head to Sibilla. They serve breakfast, lunch and dinner at affordable prices. *Daily 8am–midnight | C/ de Blanquerna 7 | tel. 9 71 20 10 03 | €–€€ | d1*

SHOPPING

Ready for a little shopping spree? Take a stroll along the stately boulevard *Passeig des Born* and then spend some time wandering up and down *Jaume III*. If you're up for more, walk up *Carrer Unió* and down *Carrer Sant Miguel*, passing Palma's best fashion stores as you go. You will find shops stocked with international designer brands as well as boutiques featuring the creations of Spanish designers. Shoes from Camper or Pretty Ballerinas by Jaime Mascaró are cheaper here than at home. Chain stores such as Zara and Mango have also opened up, so you're sure to find something to buy whatever your budget may be.

ART GALLERIES

The art scene on the island is lively and vibrant. Here's a selection from over the 30 galleries in Palma: *Altair (C/ Sant Jaume 23); Casal Solleric (Passeig* des Born 27); Sa Nostra (C/ Concepció 12); Sala Pelaires (C/ Can Verí 3). The

INSIDER TIP
A night in many museums

island's largest arts event takes place over the third weekend in September: the *Nit de l'Art*. A whole night is dedicated to art in around 25 galleries, along with live music in the streets and a range of culinary treats on offer.

CAFÈS LLOFRIU

A paradise for coffee nuts. Sniff and taste your way through more than 30 different kinds of coffee! The café has been freshly grinding beans from the gourmet Mercat d'Olivar opposite since 1866. Make sure you try the house blend. *Mon–Sat 8.30am–2pm and Mon–Fri 5–8pm | C/ Josep Tous i Ferrer 10 | e3*

COLMADO SANTO DOMINGO

Photogenic little shop in Palma's historic quarter selling *sobrasadas, jamón serrano* and other specialities. *Mon–Fri 10.15am–8pm, Sat 10.15am–7.45pm | C/ Santo Domingo 1 | c5*

COME IN

An excellent English bookshop stocking new titles as well as books about the island. *Mon–Fri 9.30am–2pm and 4–8pm, Sat 10am–2pm | C/ Sant Miquel 58 | tel. 9 71 71 16 93 | d3*

ESPECIAS CRESPI

Oriental aromas emerge from Mallorca's most famous spice shop. Over 150 different types of herbs and spices are sold by the packet, from basic oregano to expensive *azafrán*

(saffron). *Mon–Sat 10am–1.30pm and Mon–Fri 4.30–8pm | Via Sindicato 64 | especiascrespi.com | e4*

ESTANC D'ES BORN

This well-stocked tobacconist on Palma's grandest street is a local institution. One of the best-value places in Europe to find top-quality cigars. *April–Sept Mon–Sat 9am–11pm, Sun 11am–7pm; Oct–March Mon–Sat 9am–9.30pm, Sun 11am–3pm | Passeig des Born 20 | c4*

SA FORMATGERIA

This tiny shop creates a quite a stink … but in the best possible way with the aromas of countless Mediterranean

The shoe brand Camper is based on Mallorca

cheeses wafting out of the door. Eat, drink and shop at the same time, with affordable degustation plates and good wines. Try the *tabla de queso* with six local cheeses (9.90 euros). *Mon–Sat 9am–9pm | C/ Oms 30 | saformatgeria.com | ▥ c2*

MIMBRERIA VIDAL

Palma's last basket weaver is still housed in the Carrer Cordería, once the centre of the city's basket industry. You will find baskets galore here in one of the oldest shops in town. The

INSIDER TIP
Woven into the fabric

shop's huge range includes chairs with woven seats and hammocks alongside the traditional Mallorcan palm baskets. The most traditional baskets are very simple with a zip or long leather straps – perfect for using as shopping or beach bags and make a great gift.

Check out the excellent street art in the shop's neighbourhood – Sa Gerreira is the centre of Mallorca's grafitti and street art scene. *Mon–Sat 9.30am–1.30pm and Mon–Fri 4.30–8.30pm | C/ Cordería 13 | mimbreriavidal.com | ▥ e4*

SPORT & ACTIVITIES

MALLORCA FREETOUR 🐾

Want to do a little tour to get to know the city better? Mallorca Freetour offer a free (please remember to tip the guide) guided walk every day from Monday to Saturday beginning in Parc de la Mar, skirting around the cathedral and its environs, and ending up at the *Plaça Espanya (▥ e2)*. The tours

begin at 11am and are offered in English, Spanish and French. The meeting point is directly opposite the tourist information centre. They also run tours of the Jewish Quarter and the cathedral *(10 euros/pers; minimum 10 people). Tel. 6 83 31 71 92 | mallorcafreetour.com*

PALMA JUMP 👾

Bouncy castles are not just for kids! Palma Jump, on the edge of the city, has 50 trampolines, a bungee basketball court and much more. Kids are allowed to jump by themselves from the age of five. Littler ones can join their parents on the family trampoline during the week. On Friday evenings there are "bouncing parties" for teenagers including DJs and disco lights! *Sun–Thu 9am–10pm, Fri until 11pm, Sat until midnight | C/ Textil 3 | plot 33 | Son Valentí business park |*

Once the sun goes down, Palma's nightlife lights up the streets

palmajump.com | 10 euros/hr, family ticket (small child and adult) 5 euros, bouncing party (2 hrs) 12 euros | ▥ F7

WELLNESS

The *GPRO Valparaiso Palace & Spa hotel (C/ Francisco Vidal Sureda 23 | tel. 9 71 40 03 00 | gprovalparaiso.com | ▥ E7)* has the biggest and best spa in Palma. They offer a full range of treatments, from massages to hydrotherapy and Ayurveda sessions. They also have several pools and a gym. A five-hour stay begins at 35 euros.

NIGHTLIFE

The cathedral, the castle and the harbour boulevard are lit up at night. The nightlife shifts up a gear after midnight in the *Sa Llotja* quarter, on the *Passeig Marítim* and in the *El Terreno*

quarter. Whether you prefer to stroll or take a taxi from club to club, Palma nights are bright and colourful.

BLUE JAZZ CLUB & SKY BAR

Head up to the seventh floor of the Hotel Saratoga for chilled-out jam sessions and happening concerts. If you want to have a drink up in the heavens and gaze out over Palma's skyline, ascend one more floor to the Sky Bar. *Music Mon, Thu–Sat from 8.30pm | Paseo Mallorca 6 | bluejazz.es | ▥ a4*

INSIDER TIP
Almost in heaven

CINE CIUTAT ☂

Film buffs have established a cooperative to keep this arthouse cinema going. Fortunately for visitors from abroad, the cinema shows excellent films in their original language (usually with Spanish subtitles)

*admission 7.50 euros, Mon 5 euros |
C/ de l'Emperadriu Eugènia 6 | cine
ciutat.org |* ▥ *F7*

JAZZ VOYEUR CLUB
It may be tiny, but it's home to Palma's
best live jazz. *Tue–Sun from 8.30pm |
C/ Apuntadores 5 | jazzvoyeurclub.com
|* ▥ *b5*

KAELUM CLUB
This cool club on the edge of Santa
Catalina is famous for its "Tardeo" parties. From October to June, revelries
begin in the afternoon (*tarde* means
afternoon in Spanish) and go on into
the night. *Mon, Thu–Sat from 11.30pm
(in winter closed Mon) | Av. Argentina 1
| FB: kaelumclubmallorca |* ▥ *E7*

LA BODEGUITA DEL MEDIO
From Palma to Havana in just one second: grab a *mojito* and dive into the
crowd! Salsa and Latino are danced
here up close and all night long. *Daily
from midnight | C/ Valseca 18 |* ▥ *b5*

LA ROSA VERMUTERÍA
Vermouth fever has hit Palma. There
are 50 kinds to try at the La Rosa
Vermutería and at its little sister, *La
Rosa Chica (C/ de Monsenyor Palmer 5)*.
Sample some together with the classic
Gilda skewers (olive, red pepper,
anchovies). However, don't stay for a
meal as the food is mediocre. *Tue–Sun
12pm–midnight, Mon from 7pm | C/
Rosa 5 | FB: larosavermuteria |* ▥ *c–d4*

MARACA CLUB
Hot, crowded and loud but full of the
joys of partying on the Mediterranean.

Often with live acts. *Tue–Sat from
10.30pm| C/ Poeta Francesc Fiol i Joan
1 | FB: Maracaclubpalma |* ▥ *F7*

TITO'S
Legendary and pretty loud super-club
boasting a glass elevator (and harbour
views). *July/Aug daily from 11pm; for
other opening times look online |
admission varies by event
30–50 euros | Passeig Marítim |
titosmallorca.com |* ▥ *E7*

AROUND PALMA

CIUTAT JARDÍ
4.5km from Palma, 10 mins by car
Especially at the weekend, locals
descend on this villa suburb east of
Palma, and it's easy to see why! It's
right by the sea with a pretty beach
and a "foodie mile" behind it lined
with excellent fish restaurants, such as
*Casa Fernando (Tue–Sun 1–4pm and
7pm–midnight | C/ Trafalgar 27 | tel.
9 71 26 54 17 | restaurantecasa
fernando.com | €€€)*; you can pick
your seafood yourself by going up to
the counter. ▥ *f8*

PLATJA DE PALMA ✈
9km from Palma, 15 mins by car
Nowhere else on the island is the tourist infrastructure as all encompassing
as on Platja de Palma. It's especially
popular with German tourists who
head for *Beach Club Six*, aka
"Ballermann" *(C/ Arenal 45a | FB:*

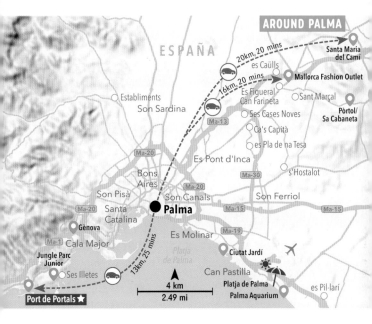

ESPAÑA

20km, 20 mins — Santa Maria del Camí

es Caülls

16km, 20 mins — Mallorca Fashion Outlet

Establiments
Son Sardina

Es Figueral
Can Farineta — Sant Marçal

Ma-13 — Ses Cases Noves — Pòrtol/ Sa Cabaneta

Ca's Capità

es Pla de na Tesa

Ma-20 — Es Pont d'Inca

Bons Aires — Ma-20 — Ma-30 — s'Hostalot

Son Pisà — Son Canals — Son Ferriol

Ma-20 — Santa Catalina — **Palma** — Ma-15 — Ma-15

Gènova — Es Molinar — Ma-19

Ma-1 — Cala Major — Platja de Palma — Ciutat Jardí

Jungle Parc Junior — 13km, 25 mins

Ses Illetes — Can Pastilla

4 km — Platja de Palma

Port de Portals ★ — 2.49 mi — Palma Aquarium — es Pil·larí

Balneario Beach Club Six Mallorca), which has been made to look like a classy Ibizan club. Right behind it, pub after bar after pub line the so-called *Bierstrasse* and *Schinkenstrasse* ("Beer" and "Ham" streets). The best time to experience this party spectacle is during the late afternoon happy hour.

The sweeping 8km sandy beach, which is divided into 16 *balnearios* (beach sections), and its palm-lined promenade, would look rather tranquil, were it not for the near-endless hotels offering tens of thousands of tourists a bed for the night. While many of the hotels have seen better days, recently a series of 4* and 5* have moved in and a collective of hoteliers has got together to rebrand the beach under the not-very-imaginative name *Palma Beach*.

The *Megapark (C/ Arenal 51 | mega park.tv/megapark)*, is a gigantic party mecca by the Ballermann hiding in a neo-Gothic edifice that can accommodate up to 8,000 partygoers. It calls itself "the largest beer garden in Europe" and its nightly musical offering hcan be found in its very large cellar. In *S'Arenal*, right at the end of the bay, young people can find good-value accommodation in simple guesthouses. *▥ G8*

PALMA AQUARIUM 👥 🏖

12.5km from Palma, 20 mins by car

There are 55 tanks, each recreating a different part of the ocean, and 8,000 marine animals in this superb aquarium. A transparent tunnel lets you get right up close to the fish, including the sharks, which you can also watch being fed. There is also a mini jungle, a Mediterranean garden, a restaurant and a café. *Daily 9.30am–6.30pm | admission 25 euros, children 14 euros | Exit 10 on the motorway (signposted at Balneario 14) | palmaaquarium.com | ⏱ 2–3 hrs | ⊞ G8*

MALLORCA FASHION OUTLET
16km from Palma, 20 mins by car
For bargain lovers a trip out to this shopping mall is a must. It houses 30 stores with over 60 well-known brands represented. ☛ The best deals are available on "Super Thursday" (the last Thursday of every month). There is also a small leisure park in the complex with mini golf, bowling, slot machines, restaurants and a multiplex cinema. *Daily 10am–10pm | Ctra. Palma–Inca, at Km7.1 | Marratxí/Sa Cabaneta exit, on the left as you leave Palma | mallorca fashionoutlet.com | ⊞ G6*

PÓRTOL/SA CABANETA
18km from Palma, 25 mins by car
This twin village (pop. 6,500) is known

for its pottery and ceramics workshops. The way to the ten *ollerías* in Pórtol – where belly-shaped *olles* and flat *greixoneras* are produced – is well signposted. *L'Albello (C/ Major 45)*, at the edge of the village, and *Sa Roca Lisa (C/ Sa Roca Lisa 24-26)* have the largest selections. The workshops of *Sa Cabaneta*, hidden in the upper part of the village, are famous for their *siu-rells* (red, white and green figurines).

Close to Sant Marçal church, *Local No 2 (in theory Mon–Sat from 7pm but opening times vary wildly so check online | C/ Casa del Poble 3 | tel. 9 71 79 79 80 | tapasmallorca.com)* serves delicious tapas – the buffet bar almost collapses under the weight of about 50 different kinds. ⊞ G6-7

SANTA MARIA DEL CAMÍ
18km from Palma, 20 mins by car
This town of 7,000 inhabitants has seen something of an invasion by British and German expats who have bought up the local fincas. Take a look at the small 17th-century cloisters,

The finest Iberico ham awaits you at Méson Can Pedro

and pay a visit to the large *Sunday market* on the new village square, where the island's organic farmers sell local fruits and vegetables, sourdough bread, ostrich salami, fig jam and more.

The craft beer brewery *Cerveza Nau (FB: Cerveza Nau)* is right in the middle of the village. From here you can explore "downtown" on foot, far away from the large main road. At the *Bar Can Beia (Wed-Mon 7-2am | C/ Oleza 4)*, on the old village square, you can sample the food all Mallorcans are raised on: mixed tapas called *variat*.

Of only two linen weavers left on the island, *Artesania Tèxtil Bujosa (C/ Bernardo Santa Eugènia 53)* is the only one to still manufacture traditional ikats by hand; this is of course reflected in the price. ⫘ *H6*

GENOVA
6km from Palma, 15 mins by car
With its many authentic cosy bars and restaurants in romantic locations among Genova's steps and wine terraces, this western suburb of Palma is foodie heaven. Rustic but great Mallorcan food can be found at *Mesón Can Pedro (daily 12.30pm-12.30am | C/ del Rector Vives 14 | tel. 9 71 70 21 62 | canpedro.es | €)* which has its very own charcoal barbecue.

For a great day out, first visit the cave complex and then talk about them over lunch at the charming but eccentric *Ses Coves de Genova (Tue-Sun 1-4pm and Thu-Sat 8pm-midnight | C/ Barranc 45 | tel. 9 71 40 23 87 | cuevasdegenova.com | €€)*; the restaurant doubles up as a ticket office for the caves. ⫘ *E7*

JUNGLE PARC JUNIOR 👻
10km from Palma, 15 mins by car
If your kids (4-11) are into running around, shrieking with joy, and testing both their courage and their brains, they will have a whale of a time in this little patch of jungle near Palma. This, a smaller version of the *Jungle Parc (Santa Ponça)*, houses six routes for little adventurers to get to grips with. Should they need any help, there are park rangers on hand with hints, clues and encouragement. *Opening times vary wildly, check the website | admission 14 euros | C/ Arquitecto Frances Casas 16 | Bendinat | jungleparcjunior. es | ⏱ 2 hrs | ⫘ E8*

PORT DE PORTALS ★
11km from Palma, 20 mins by car
The exclusive marina below Portals Nous acts like a magnet for all who want to see and be seen. Mooring fees are among the most expensive on the island, and the harbour boulevard with its high-end boutiques and expensive restaurants reflect this. *Diablito (daily 9am-midnight | tel. 9 71 67 65 03 | €€)* is mainly frequented by young people ordering huge pizzas. *Wellie's (daily 9am-midnight | tel. 8 71 90 23 06 | €€)* is the (overpriced) meeting place for an evening *copa* (or drink); it also serves opulent salad platters. If you want to "eat Mallorcan" but can't afford the prices in Fernando P. Arellano's 2-star Michelin restaurant, you'll find cheaper options at his bistro 🐟 *Baiben (daily 1-3.30pm and 7-10.30pm | Locales 1-6 | tel. 9 71 67 55 47 | baiben restaurants.com/en). ⫘ E8)*

THE WEST

BREATHTAKINGLY BEAUTIFUL

Big resorts and solitary coastal walks. The west can offer both.
The stunning Serra de Tramuntana coastline has some of the
most spectacular scenery on Mallorca. If you don't have the
time to enjoy the beauty of this region on a hike, you should at
least drive a section of the coastal road, Ma10.

While the area in the far southwest around Andratx and Peguera
has been somewhat spoiled by over-development, the wonderfully
untouched villages of Estellencs and Banyalbufar can be found

Bird's-eye view of Cala Fonoll near Andratx on Mallorca's west coast

hidden along the steep coast. They are accessible via long, winding roads with hairpin bends that offer surprising glimpses of old watchtowers, lemon plantations, olive groves and terrace farms along the way.

The popular villages of Valldemossa, Deià and Sóller have also retained their original appeal, while Fornalutx has gone one step further and been crowned Spain's most beautiful village.

THE WEST

MARCO POLO HIGHLIGHTS

★ **SA DRAGONERA**
The place is teeming with small lizards –
are these the "dragons" that gave the
protected island its name? ➤ p. 64

★ **BANYALBUFAR/ESTELLENCS**
Beautiful paths take you down from the
idyllic villages on the slopes of the
Tramuntana mountains to glorious
swimming coves ➤ p. 65

★ **VALLDEMOSSA'S LOWER VILLAGE**
Stroll along flower-lined streets, follow
in the footsteps of a saint – and enjoy
the delicious potato doughnuts that sell
like hot cakes ➤ p. 66

★ **SÓLLER VALLEY**
Protected by mighty mountain peaks
and adorned by flowering trees:
welcome to the Valley of the Oranges!
➤ p. 69

★ **FORNALUTX**
Even climbing all the steps is a joy in
Fornalutx, said to be Mallorca's prettiest
mountain village ➤ p. 72

★ **TORRENT DE PAREIS**
Regardless of how you get there, this
canyon is a marvel of nature ➤ p. 72

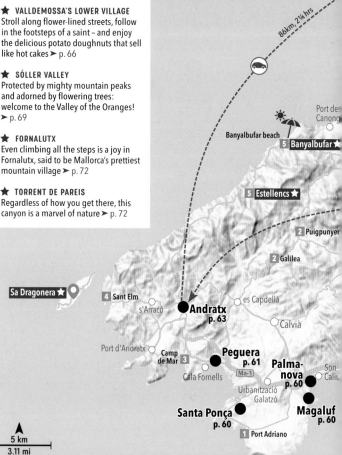

86km, 2¼ hrs

Port des
Canong

Banyalbufar beach

5 Banyalbufar ★

5 Estellencs ★

2 Puigpunyer

2 Galilea

Sa Dragonera ★

4 Sant Elm

s'Arracó

es Capdellà

Andratx
p. 63

Calvià

Port d'Andratx

Camp
de Mar 3

Peguera
p. 61

Palma-
nova
p. 60

Son
Caliu

Cala Fornells

Ma-1

Urbanització
Galatzó

Magaluf
p. 60

Santa Ponça
p. 60

1 Port Adriano

5 km
3.11 mi

Cala de sa Calobra | **14** Torrent de Pareis ★

Lluc

Port de Sóller

12 Mirador de Ses Barques

11 Fornalutx ★

13 Embalse de Cúber

Sóller
p. 70

10 Lluc Alcari

Caimari

Selva

Son Marroig 9

Deià
p. 68

● Sóller Valley ★

Mancor de la Vall

Biniamar

6 Ermita de la Trinitat

16 Orient

7 Port de Valldemossa

Lloseta

Inca

Valldemossa
p. 65

Alaró

Valldemossa's lower village ★ **15** Bunyola

Binissalem

Ma-11

50km, 45 mins

Consell

Ma-13

Santa Maria
del Camí

8 Esporles

Sencelles

Cas Canar

Biniali

es Caülls

Establiments

Ses Cases
Noves

● Es Figueral - Can Farineta

Sant Marçal

Ca's Capità

es Pla de na Tesa

Pòrtol

Santa Eugènia

Pina

Ma-20

Ma-30

s'Hostalot

Ma-20

Palma

Ma-15

Son Gual

Algaida

Ma-19

ndinat

es Pil-larí

Randa

Ses Cadenes
Bellavista

Llucmajor

PALMANOVA/ MAGALUF/ SANTA PONÇA

(*III D8*) **This huge resort conglomerate consisting of Palmanova, Magaluf and Santa Ponça belongs to Calvià, whose 50,000 inhabitants form part of the island's second-largest municipality, and one of the wealthiest in Europe.**

The wealth stems from tourism and the tax revenues of rich finca owners. The massive, conjoined hotels, pubs and snack bars are fairly faceless. The beaches, however, are long, wide and pretty. This is British Partyville (similar to German Party-Stadt in west Palma).

EATING & DRINKING

CIRO'S

Long-established large restaurant, with a terrace and sea views and good Mediterranean cuisine. *Daily noon–midnight | Paseo del Mar 3 | Palmanova | tel. 9 71 68 10 52 | www.restauranteciros.es | daily | €€*

SPORT & ACTIVITIES

JUNGLE PARC 😕

Various levels of difficulty have to be overcome as you work your way through the tree-canopy climbing course in the pine forest. Both children and adults will get their money's worth. *Daily 10am–6.30pm | admission from 14 euros | Av. del Rei Jaume I 40 | Santa Ponça | jungleparc.es | 2 hrs*

KATMANDU PARK 😕

An American-influenced adventure park for kids, but with added fear factor. One of the main attractions is the House of Katmandu, a brightly painted upside-down house, which is more than a little spooky. Its eight rooms are all dark and themed – there is a torture chamber and a room with a yeti. The short films in the 5D cinema are not for the faint hearted. And there are climbing walls in case you want to build up some endorphins. *April–June and mid-Sept–Nov daily 10am–6pm, July–mid-Sept daily 10am–10pm | day passes and multi-day tickets available (check website for prices) | Av. Pedro Vaquer Ramis 9 | at the Magaluf Park Hotel | Magaluf | katmandupark.com | 4–6 hrs*

WESTERN WATER PARK 😕

This lively water park trumps the neighbouring Aquaparc, thanks to its Western show and breathtaking tower dives. *Daily 10am–5pm, in high season 10am–6pm | admission 30 euros, children (5–10) 21 euros, online booking is cheaper | Ctra. Cala Figuera a Sa Porrasa | Magaluf | www.westernpark.com | 4–6 hrs*

NIGHTLIFE

The nightlife here is a bit too geared towards the cut-price hotels in the area. Youngsters tend to enjoy the super-club *BCM (May–Oct daily 10pm–6am | Magaluf)*.

If you feel like dancing, head to BCM Planet Dance in Magaluf

AROUND SANTA PONÇA

🔳 PORT ADRIANO

5km from the Santa Ponça motorway exit (well signposted), 10 mins by car

The cool and unadorned concrete, glass and stainless-steel modern architecture of the harbour is accentuated by its luxury yachts and exclusive shops and restaurants. Unfortunately, the view of the sea is blocked by a protective wall. However, you can admire the huge boats in the port and there are regular festivals and events, including street food festivals and concerts by the likes of José Carreras. *portadriano.com* | 📖 *C9*

PEGUERA

(📖 C8) **The seaside resort of Peguera (pop. 3,900) is particularly popular with German visitors, and it's easy to see why, with beautiful hiking routes and dreamy mountain villages in its hilly hinterland.**

This has led to a bustling tourist industry and the village has also gained from seeing its former main road turned into a pedestrianised promenade. Along the *Bulevar* you will find bars and restaurants, boutiques and souvenir shops, mostly catering for German tourists. Peguera was once a bastion of so-called hibernators or long-term vacationers. Today, some younger visitors, drawn to activity holidays, flock to the island's largest tennis centre (the venue for

Gain a new perspective at CCA Andratx

the *Mallorca Open*) or to one of the five golf courses in the vicinity. The beaches, however, are fairly small considering the number of visitors Peguera receives.

EATING & DRINKING

MAR Y MAR

The fish restaurant directly on the beach offers an extensive menu with fish and seafood, soups, snacks and salads together with a sea view and a relaxed atmosphere. *C/ Pinaret 6 | tel. 9 71 94 62 08 | www.marymar-mallorca.com | daily | €€-€€€*

NIGHTLIFE

DISCOTECA RENDEZVOUS

A very long and well-stocked bar which, with its 60s style, is geared towards the older clubbing clientele.

On the main promenade. *Daily 10pm-5am | FB: RendezvousPaguera*

AROUND PEGUERA

☑ GALILEA/PUIGPUNYENT

Galilea: 15km from Peguera, 30 mins by car. Puigpunyent: 30km, 45 mins.

Galilea's biblical name suggests a blissful retreat. The airy terraced village (pop. 290) serves as an idyllic second home to many foreigners whose houses offer fine views towards the sea. Good pizza and pasta are served at the *Trattoria Galilea (daily 11am-11pm | tel. 6 39 38 37 65 | €€-€€€)*. For a slightly cheaper and much more Spanish restaurant try *Can Andreu (Tue-Thu 10am-9pm, Fri-Sun 10am-11pm | tel. 9 71 61 41 87 | FB: Ca-n-Andreu-Restaurant | €€)*, which has a charming terrace and views of the church.

A small pass around 4km long divides Galilea and *Puigpunyent* (pop. 1,400). One of the fine old estates dotted around the village has been converted by its American owner into a fairly ostentatious hotel. Inside you will find *Oleum (daily May-Sept 7.30-10.30pm, Oct-April 7-10.15pm | tel. 9 71 14 70 00 | sonnet.es | €€€)*, its restaurant, whose furnishings include an impressive 17th-century oil press! The hotel also has its own treehouse for special occasions. You can eat up there at a lofty altitude of 4m. ◫ *D6*

ANDRATX

(□ C7) **In the shade of a sturdy fortified church, framed by pine-covered hills, the country town of Andratx (pop. 6,300) is more or less permanently having a siesta.**

Apart from on Wednesdays when there's a market on, you won't meet many tourists here; they prefer the extremely built-up harbour town *Port d'Andratx* (pop. 3,000), 5km away.

SIGHTSEEING

CCA ANDRATX

The 4,000m² space of this art gallery houses exhibitions of nationally and internationally significant contemporary art. *March–Oct Tue–Fri 10.30am-7pm, Sat/Sun until 4pm, Nov–Feb Tue–Sun 10.30am-4pm | admission 8 euros | about 1km outside town towards Es Capdellà | C/ Estanyera 2 | ccandratx.com | ⏱ 1hr*

STUDIO WEIL

A futuristic building whose strange geometric shapes can't help but grab your attention at the end of the harbour road leading to La Mola. It was designed by the world-famous architect Daniel Libeskind for Barbara Weil, the painter and sculptor who died in 2018. *Studio Weil | open by appointment only | Camí de Sant Carles 20 | Port d'Andratx | studioweil.com*

CALA LLAMP/SA MOLA

Check out the level of (nouveau) richness in such a small area! The hilly backcountry between the *Sa Mola* peninsula and the steep coast above the cliff-fringed bay of *Cala Llamp* is full of crazily luxurious villas.

EATING & DRINKING

The harbour town of Port d'Andratx has one of the largest fishing fleets of the island. Don't consider leaving without enjoying some local fish – even though the prices are admittedly steep. The restaurants *Can Pep (daily 12.30-11pm | C/ Mateo Bosch 30a | tel. 9 71 61 95 91 | restaurantcanpep. com | €€-€€€), Rocamar (daily 12pm-midnight | Av. Almirante Riera Alemany 27 | tel. 9 71 67 12 61 | www.rocamar.eu | €€-€€€)* and *Miramar (daily 12-3.30pm and 7.30-11.30pm | Av. Mateo Bosch 18 | tel. 9 71 67 19 23 | miramarpuertoadratx. com | €€-€€€)* make the investment even more worthwhile because of the sea view you can enjoy along with it.

OLIU

The quality of the olives that are used for the canapés says a lot about the garden restaurant of young Mallorcan Joan Porcel. He is obsessed with the finest of details and cooks divine food, no matter whether you order fish, vegetables or dessert. *Tue–Sun 1-4pm and 7-11pm | Ctra. Port d'Andratx 67 | tel. 9 71 23 58 30 | oliu.es | €€-€€€*

VILLA ITALIA

This villa (now a hotel) sits regally atop a hill above the harbour. There is a restaurant and cocktail bar, and the lunch menu is a finger-licking bargain

Green shutters and pot plants embellish the alleyways of Valldemossa

at 29 euros. You'd pay that for the harbour views alone. *Daily 12.30–3pm and 7–10pm | Camí Sant Carles 13 | tel. 9 71 67 40 11 | hotelvillaitalia. com | €€–€€€*

AROUND ANDRATX

3 CAMP DE MAR
4km from Andratx, 10 mins by car
A wooded bendy road with pretty views connects Port d'Andratx with Camp de Mar, a place which over the past few years has seen much development and become quite a refined place to stay on Mallorca. If you are into golf, the *Golf de Andratx* course is an ideal place to tee off *(green fees from 80 euros | golfdeandratx.com)* | *C8*

4 SANT ELM
8km from Andratx, 20 mins by car
The best thing about the small seaside resort of Sant Elm (pop. 400) is its tranquillity – and the view of the offshore island of ★ *Sa Dragonera*. In summer, Sa Dragonera can be reached by the ferry *Margarita* in about 20 minutes *(Feb–Oct Mon–Sat from 9.45am; last return Feb–March and Oct 3pm, April–Sept 4.50pm | tickets 13 euros | tel. 6 39 61 75 45 | crucerosmargarita. com)*. The strictly protected islet, 4.2km long, up to 1km wide has a natural history museum and hiking trails, and is home to endemic lizards and many types of bird.

From Sant Elm, not one but three hiking trails lead to the monastery of *Sa Trapa* (with a refuge managed by the GOB – Grup Balear d'Ornitologia I Defensa de la Naturalesa). The cosy *Na Caragola* restaurant *(daily 9.30am–11pm | tel. 9 71 23 90 06 |*

restaurantenacaragola.com | €€), with terrace above the old harbour, serves good Mediterranean fare. *A–B7*

5 BANYALBUFAR/ESTELLENCS ★

Banyabulfar 25km from Andratx, 40 mins by car; Estellencs 18km from Andratx, 30 mins by car

These two rock-solid villages of Arabic origin cling to a mountain high above the sea. Situated on the winding Ma10 coastal road along elegant terraces dating back to Moorish times, they are best explored on foot – be prepared for lots of steps.

Banyalbufar has a population of just 500 but still has plenty of bars and restaurants. The classics are *Son Tomas (Wed–Mon 12.30–3.30pm and 7.30–9.45pm | tel. 9 71 61 81 49 | €€)* and *1661 Cuina de Banyalbufar (daily 10am–midnight | tel. 9 71 61 82 45 | €€). Estellencs* is the same size and has a lovely villagey feel. Both villages have beaches (signposted) where pretty waterfalls double up as natural showers. Banyalbufar beach is rocky but very pretty indeed. *D5–6*

VALLDEMOSSA

(E5) **Coming up from Palma on the winding road, the view of the mountain village of Valldemossa (pop. 1,950) will leave you speechless – especially when the almond trees are in bloom.**

The summer palace King Jaume II had built here was extended by his son and successor Sancho I. Today, the narrow houses with flowering gardens, crowned by the parish church and the monastery, continue to enthral visitors.

SIGHTSEEING

REAL CARTUJA

Every year, over 300,000 tourists shuffle through this monastery on the trail of Frédéric Chopin and George Sand who spent six cold and wet weeks here in winter 1838–39. Before 10.30am and after 4pm you can admire everything in peace and quiet. From 1399 until 1835, the former royal residence was a Carthusian monastery. The building we see today dates from the 18th century. The old monastic pharmacy is well worth seeing, as is the exhibition on Archduke Ludwig Salvator with pieces from his estate and a lot of information on the life of this Mallorca enthusiast. Don't miss the *Palau de Rei Sanxo* either, for its fine furnishings and occasional short piano concerts. *Feb–Oct Mon–Sat 10am–4.30pm, Nov–Jan closed | admission 8.50 euros | cartujadelvalldemossa.com | 1.5–2.5 hrs*

INSIDER TIP
Beat the crowds

FUNDACIÓ CULTURAL COLL BARDOLET

The most enchanting works in this gallery set up after the death of Coll Bardolet, the Catalan painter who lived in Valldemossa up to his death in 2007, are the paintings depicting dancing scenes. He was a significant artist, so it is pleasing that this

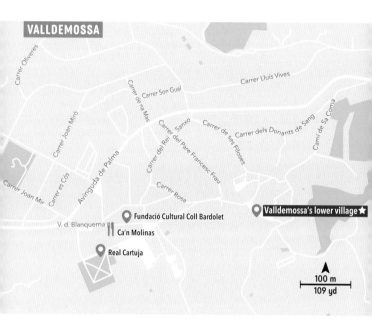

VALLDEMOSSA

Carrer Oliveres · Carrer Joan Miró · Carrer de na Mas · Carrer Son Gual · Carrer Lluís Vives · Carrer del Rei Sanxo · Carrer del Pare Francesc Frau · Carrer de ses Filoses · Carrer dels Donants de Sang · Camí de Sa Coma · Carrer Joan Mir · Carrer es Cos · Avinguda de Palma · Carrer Rosa

V. d. Blanquerna

📍 Fundació Cultural Coll Bardolet

🍴 Ca'n Molinas

📍 Real Cartuja

📍 Valldemossa's lower village ★

100 m
109 yd

foundation has found a worthy home on the main street. *April–Oct Mon–Fri 10am–7pm, Sat 10am–2pm and 4–7pm, Sun 10am–8pm; Nov–March Tue–Sat 10am–4pm, Sun 10am–2pm and 3–6pm | admission free | C/ Blanquerna 4 | fccollbardolet.org |* 🕐 *40 mins*

VALLDEMOSSA'S LOWER VILLAGE ★

No other island village is adorned with as many flowers as Valldemossa's lower village. It has a beautiful Gothic church dedicated Sant Bartomeu, while the decorative tiles on every house depict scenes from the life of Santa Catalina, born in Carrer Rectoría. The former maidservant Catalina Tomàs (1531–74) has been honoured with a charming monument next to the parish church. Mallorcans drive for miles to see her – and to buy *cocas de patata*, potato doughnuts available in any bakery here.

EATING & DRINKING

CA'N MOLINAS

This bakery and its beautiful garden are almost 100 years old. A *café con leche* will never taste the same again after you've enjoyed one here in the shade of the garden's trees. And it will taste even better with a couple of their scrumptious almond biscuits. Or, of course, a *coca de patata. Daily 9am–7.30pm | C/ Blanquerna 15 | canmolinas.com | €*

INSIDER TIP
A green oasis

AROUND VALLDEMOSSA

6 ERMITA DE LA TRINITAT 🚩

3km from Valldemossa, 5 mins by car
Founded in 1648, the tiny hermitage has a stupendous sea view. Hermits live here to this day, following the rules of saints Paul and Anthony. The car is best left in the car park below; the romantic if narrow and bendy road can be tackled on foot (around 20 mins). *About 3km north on the Deià road, the narrow entry to the driveway is easy to miss. It is directly opposite the Can Costa restaurant |* 🕐 *30 mins |* ⌕ *E5*

7 PORT DE VALLDEMOSSA

8km from Valldemossa, 20 mins by car
Tiny and romantic, this pebbly harbour bay is a great place to go swimming and is reached after 8km of hairpin bends (*signposted turn-off from the Ma10*). (Nervous drivers should avoid this – the only – access road!) Try the *Es Port* beach tavern *(daily 10am–9.30pm | C/ Ponent 5 | tel. 9 71 61 61 94 | restaurantesport.es | €€)* on the nicely restored harbour. ⌕ *E5*

8 ESPORLES

15km from Valldemossa, 20 mins by car
The long, sprawling village of Esporles (pop. 4,940) with its 🚩 lively village square lies in a fertile, evergreen valley southwest of Valldemossa. Situated around 1.5km north of Esporles, the country estate of *La Granja (daily 10am–7pm, winter opening times can vary | admission 15 euros (incl. tasting) | tel. 9 71 61 00 32 | lagranja.net|* 🕐 *2–2.5 hrs)* dates back to Roman and Moorish times. Since the 1970s the place has been an open-air museum housing workshops as well as replicas of aristocratic salons. Its torture chamber will bring even the hardiest out in goosebumps. On Wednesdays and Fridays there are performances of regional dances and a horse show. ⌕ *E6*

DEIÀ

(⌕ F4) **Over half of the 640 inhabitants of this picture-perfect hill village are foreigners. In the 1920s, Deià attracted the artists; today it's wealthy finca owners.**

Hotels and restaurants have followed suit. In summer, long lines of traffic try to push through the narrow street leading through the village, and the romantic pebble beach of *Cala de Deià* is overrun with visitors.

SIGHTSEEING

CHURCH HILL

Enchanting narrow streets and flights of steps lead up to the church and its cemetery, which has great views. One of the artists who found their last resting place here is the British writer Robert Graves (1895–1985). His fictionalised biography *I, Claudius* was written in Deià, where he lived for over

40 years. A small *museum (April–Oct Mon–Fri 10am–4.20pm, Sat 10am–2.20pm, Nov–March Mon–Fri 9am–4pm, Sat 9am–2pm. Opening times vary so check the website | admission 7 euros | lacasaderobertgraves.org | ⏱ 1 hr)* is dedicated to him.

EATING & DRINKING

ES RACÓ D'ES TEIX

You will eat like an emperor above the roofs of Deiá if you splash out 115 euros on the seven-course set meal prepared by culinary conjuror Josef Sauerschell. *Tue–Sun 1–3pm and 7.30–10.30pm | C/ de sa Vinya Vella 6 | tel. 9 71 63 95 01 | esracodesteix.es | €€€*

LA RESIDENCIA

This former manor house, framed by cascades of blossoms and with dreamy views of the church hill is now a hotel with a gourmet restaurant called *El Olivo (daily 7.30am–10.30pm | tel. 9 71 63 60 46 | hotel-laresidencia. com | €€€)*. In the summer you can sit on the patio and look up at the stars. Their guided picnics, with their very own donkeys carrying the baskets, are a huge hit. The baskets are filled with Mallorcan delicacies (cheese, wine and olives) and the donkeys will trudge to great heights in the mountains so you can enjoy your food with an incredible view.

INSIDER TIP
Picnic with Eeyore

NIGHTLIFE

Tourists, the in-crowd and artists – in short, everybody – meets in Deià's *Café sa Fonda (Tue–Sun 1–3pm and 7.30–10.30pm | C/Arxiduc Luís Salvador 3)*. One regular is a grandson of Robert Graves, who helps to organise the eco-logical arts festival *Posidonia*

Climb aboard the tram for a holiday ride through Sóller

(*posidoniamallorca.org*); the festival aims to use the arts, music and film to connect with older cultural traditions.

AROUND DEIÀ

9 SON MARROIG

3.5km from Deià, 10 mins by car

The former retirement residence of Archduke Ludwig Salvator (see p. 18) is today a museum. Its idyllic gardens alone make a visit worthwhile. With the permission of the gatekeeper, you can take the private road to the *Sa Foradada* peninsula where the archduke anchored his yacht in 1867 and first set foot on Mallorcan soil. In summer the *restaurant* in the *Mirador (tel. 9 71 63 60 84 | €-€€)* is open from 1–10pm (in winter call ahead to see if they're open). Be sure to order the paella prepared over a wood fire. It is every bit as good as the view from the restaurant. *Mon–Sat April–Oct 9.30am–6pm, Nov–March 9am–5pm | admission 4 euros | On the Ma10 at Km65.5 | ⏱ 1.5–2hrs | ⧉ E4*

> **INSIDER TIP**
> **Perfectly prepared paella**

10 LLUC ALCARI

3km from Deià, 10 mins by car

This much-photographed village of natural stone above the sea only has 13 inhabitants. There are a couple of houses, some guard towers and a large hotel. As such, it is one of the last places to see Mallorca as it was 100 years ago. In the *Bens d'Avall* restaurant *(Tue–Sun 1–3pm and Wed–Sat 7–10pm | tel. 9 71 63 23 81 | bensdavall.com | €€€)* you can feast on the finest Mediterranean cuisine on an enchanting terrace high above the sea. To get there, drive for around 6km along a bendy road signposted to Sóller. ⧉ F4

SÓLLER

(⧉ G4) **The narrow-guage railway connecting the town of Sóller (pop. 14,000) to Palma is more than a hundred years old.**

The 50-minute trip on the 🚋 *Ferrocarril de Sóller (return ticket 25 euros, children 3–6 12.50 euros | trendesoller.com)* through 13 tunnels into the ⭐ *Sóller Valley* is particularly attractive between October and May when the oranges are ripening. Mighty high mountain peaks protect the vast swathes of orange and lemon trees growing in the valley basin, and lure hikers to explore the varied mountain paths. The views over Sóller, with its elegant art nouveau houses and pretty market square, are stunning. One particularly pleasant walk is the circular route Sóller–Fornalutx–Biniaraix–Sóller.

In town, a tram with open-topped carriages *(ticket 7 euros)* makes its gentle way from Sóller to the newly spruced-up port, about 5km away. For car drivers, access to Sóller is through a tunnel or over the mountain via a more interesting, but stomach-churning narrow road of hairpin bends.

SIGHTSEEING

JARDÍ BOTÀNIC DE SÓLLER

Located on the outskirts of Sóller, this highly informative garden houses and exhibits plants not only native to the island but from across the whole Mediterranean and the Canary Islands. *Mon-Sat March-Oct 10am-6pm; Nov-Feb 10am-2pm | admission 8 euros | Exit at Km30.5 on the country road between Palma and Port de Sóller | jardibotanicdesoller.org | ◷ 1.5 hrs*

OIL MILLS

Only three specific types of olives may be used to make the particularly pure *Oli de Mallorca*. The olives harvested around Sóller are considered some of the best on the island and the town possesses two *tafonas* (oil mills) that admit visitors. One of these belongs to the *Cooperativa Agricola Sant Bartomeu (Ctra. de Fornalutx 8)* on the road from Sóller to Fornalutx. They produce the top-quality *Oli d'Oliva Verge*. You can buy souvenirs at the cooperative's visitor centre, the *Capvespre (Mon-Fri 9am-2pm | centre capvespre.com)* where you can also join guided tours of the valley's olive and orange growers. The town's second olive mill is *La Almazara de Can Det (Carrer d'Ozones 8 | candet.es).*

ECOVINYASSA

More than 2,500 citrus trees grow on this idyllically situated organic finca. In the exhibition are informative displays about oranges and lemons. At the end, a glass of fresh orange juice and a *pa amb oli* await. *Mon, Wed, Fri 10am-2pm; Nov-early Feb closed | admission 12 euros (booking required) | Ctra. Fornalutx-Sóller | tel. 6 15 17 27 59 | ecovinyassa.com | ◷ 1.5 hrs*

EATING & DRINKING

The quality of the restaurants on the harbour boulevard varies and the prices are often exorbitant. If you are set on dinner with an ocean view, head to *Sa Barca (daily 12-10.30pm; Nov-Feb closed | Passeig Es Través 19 | tel. 9 71 63 99 43 | sabarcasoller.com | €€-€€€)* and try the carpaccio with *Sóller gambas*, or give *Randemar* a go *(daily 12pm-midnight; closed Nov-early March | Passeig Es Través 16 | tel. 9 71 63 45 78 | €€-€€€).*

AGAPANTO

A lovely setting right by the sea on the Platja d'en Repic and a charming host in the shape of Ana Maria Sturm. The herby rack of Mallorcan lamb is very good. *Thu-Tue 12pm-midnight | Camino del Faro 2 | Port de Sóller | tel. 9 71 63 38 60 | agapanto.com | €€*

JUMEIRAH

Treat yourself for once. This five-star hotel clings to the top of the cliffs above the harbour like a bird's nest Order yourself a drink at the bar in the *Sunset Sushi Lounge* and then find a spot near one of the huge windows. Sip away as the sun slips below the horizon. *Wed-Sun 5pm-1am | C/ Bélgica | Port de Sóller | tel. 9 71 63 78 88 | jumeirah.com | €€€*

INSIDER TIP
Sundowner spot

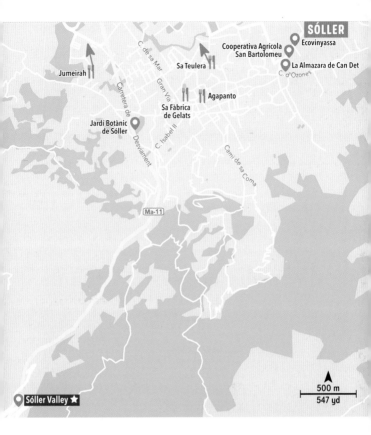

SA FÀBRICA DE GELATS
This ice-cream shop is famous across the island. Over 40 flavours and a pretty patio. *Opposite the market hall*

SA TEULERA
Renovated but rustic and serving up Mallorcan food for a fair price – no matter whether you treat yourself to the suckling pig or opt for the menu of the day. *Daily 10am–10pm | Ctra. Sóller–Puig Major | 2.5km from Sóller towards Fornalutx | tel. 9 71 63 11 11 | www.sateulera.es | €–€€*

SHOPPING
On the narrow shopping street, *C/ de sa Lluna*, you will find well-stocked retailers offering leather goods *(no. 46)*, shoes *(no. 74)*, local crafts including jewellery and bags made in Sóller *(no. 43)* or delicious pastries *(no. 95)*. Be sure to buy some of the sumptuous Sóller Chutney at Colmado La Luna *(no. 3)*. Made from lemons, oranges and aubergines, it's a snip at 6 euros a jar.

INSIDER TIP
Scrummy chutney!

AROUND SÓLLER

🔟 FORNALUTX ★

4km from Sóller, 15 mins by car

Above Sóller sits the pretty village of Fornalutx (pop. 660). So lovely, in fact, that it has been crowned the prettiest village on the island many times. Stroll through its stepped lanes lined with flowers and ochre-coloured stone houses before enjoying a freshly squeezed orange juice on the market square. Why do so many houses in the village have painted roof tiles? To find out, visit the 🐦 *Can Xoroi (Fri/Sat*

Pretty: Fornalutx

10.30am–1.30pm | admission free | (C/ de Sa Font 8 | www.canxoroi.com | ⏱ 40 mins). Located in the former oil mill, this museum of local history and culture will explain many of the village's idiosyncrasies. At the restaurant *La Cuina d'en Marc (Tue–Sun 12.30–3pm and 7.30–10.30pm | C/ Arbona Colom 6 | tel. 9 71 63 98 64 | lacuinadenmarc. com | €€)*, Marc Martinez, a young, creative chef, transforms regional products into delightful dishes. 🗺 *G4*

🔢 MIRADOR DE SES BARQUES

8km from Sóller, 15 mins by car

This enchanting viewpoint with *restaurant (Tue–Sat 10am–4pm and 7–10.30pm, Sun 10am–6pm | tel. 9 71 63 07 92 | €€)* situated above Sóller, commands magnificent panoramic views of Port de Sóller (our tip: try the suckling pig). From Mirador de ses Barques, a pretty (but not unchallenging) trail takes you to *Cala Tuent* beach in around four hours, leaving you ready to dive into the blue water. 🗺 *G4*

🔢 EMBALSE DE CÚBER

19km from Sóller, 30 mins by car

Together with the neighbouring *Embalse de Gorg Blau*, this reservoir below Puig Major supplies Palma with drinking water. Make sure to glance up to the skies when visiting. With any luck, vultures will be circling above you. The majestic but endangered black vulture is Europe's largest bird with a wingspan of 2.95m. 🗺 *G–H4*

🔢 TORRENT DE PAREIS ★

36km from Sóller, 1 hr by car

The car journey to the mouth of the

Torrent de Pareis is 14km of hairpin bends, through narrow gates formed from the rock and with great sea views. Alternatively, a one-hour boat trip from Port de Sóller takes you past dramatic rocky cliffs. The challenging climbing expedition from Escorca through the 4-km canyon of the Torrent de Pareis takes over six hours and should only be attempted by experienced hikers. It ends at the scree-lined mouth of the wild brook, also accessible from Sa Calobra through two pedestrian tunnels. A sky-high rocky arch reveals a view of the sea across the pebble beach as the craggy rocks of the canyon lie behind you. Bring a picnic basket with you and find a spot on the *Cala de sa Calobra* beach. Expect crowds. Very early in the morning and after about 5pm, it is much quieter and more pleasurable for both swimming and admiring the landscape. *H3*

INSIDER TIP
The early bird

At the roundabout before the tunnel heading to Sóller, a road full of hairpin bends branches off and leads through olive and almond groves to the mountain pass (about a 15-minute drive). Here, at the restaurant *Dalt des Coll (Wed–Sun 11am–5pm, evenings reservations only | Ctra. Palma Sóller, Km22 | tel. 9 71 61 53 80 | €€)*, you can almost always feast on freshly baked almond cake. The pretty Arabian-style park *Jardins d'Alfabia (March–April daily 9.30am–6.30pm, last admission 5.30pm | admission 7.50 euros | Km17 on the Ma11 | jardinesdealfabia.com | 1½ hrs)* is located on the road back to Sóller. The historic *Raixa family estate (Tue–Sat 10am–3pm | admission free | Km12 on the Ma11 | 1½ hrs)* has recently been restored and opened to the public. The huge park and the buildings, designed in the 18th/19th centuries by Cardinal Antonio Despuig, house an exhibit on the Tramuntana Mountains World Heritage Site. *F5*

15 BUNYOLA

10km from Sóller, 15 mins by car

An idyllic village without any major sightseeing highlights where the village square is the heart of the action. *Els Fogons de Plaça (daily 9am–4pm | next to the town hall | tel. 9 71 14 84 92)* sells excellent takeaway food. For delicious ingredients, visit the organic shop *Herbes i Paraules (Mon–Sat 10am–1.30pm and 5–8pm | C/ Sant Mateu 4 | tel. 9 71 14 83 16 | www.herbesiparaules.com)* near the main square selling almonds, wine and honey and, if you order in advance, local fruit and vegetables.

16 ORIENT

25km from Sóller, 1 hr by car

In the middle of beautiful orchards lies the remote and picturesque village of Orient (pop. 30). If you are hungry, head to the very good restaurant of the hotel *L'Hermitage (daily 7.30–10.30pm, Nov–mid-March closed | tel. 9 71 18 03 03 | hermitage-hotel.com | €€€)*, housed in a former monastery.

The *Comassema Estate (tour 25 euros/pers | itinerem.com | 2½–3 hrs)* in the Orient valley allows you to see how the nobility lived in the 16th century and what kind of work took place on these grand estates. *F–G5*

THE NORTH

ANCIENT, WILD & EXCITING

Ancient Roman cities, scenery that never ceases to surprise and an almost untouched natural paradise. Even inveterate Mallorca experts find themselves speechless every time they visit the Formentor peninsula, the northernmost tip of the island. It might be the constant interplay of light and colour that occurs here, or the astonishing scenery around Lluc monastery, tucked away high up in the Serra de Tramuntana, or one of the many other amazing aspects of Mallorca's north.

Light and shade at Cape Formentor

Around every bend you will discover impressive panoramas with rugged rock faces, finca oases and a deep-blue ocean. It's a paradise, and not only for swimmers, hikers and cyclists. The history of the Mediterranean island is still very much alive in the ancient Roman cities and medieval castles of this region. Meanwhile, modern life pulses in the major tourist centres around the bays of Alcúdia and Cala Rajada.

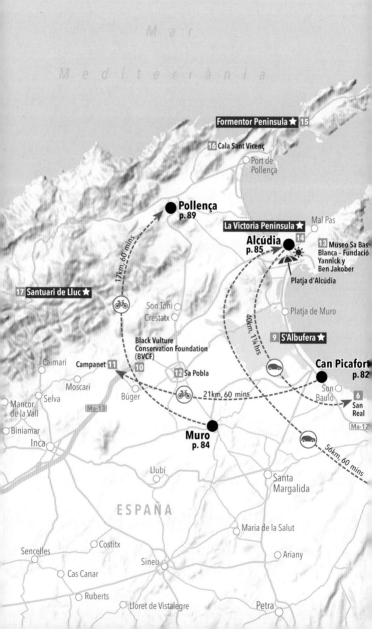

THE NORTH

Mar
Mediterrània

Formentor Peninsula ★ 15

16 Cala Sant Vicenç

Port de
Pollença

Pollença
p. 89

Mal Pas

La Victoria Peninsula ★

Alcúdia
p. 85

14

13 Museo Sa Bas-
Blanca – Fundació
Yannick y
Ben Jakober

Platja d'Alcúdia

17 Santuari de Lluc ★

171km, 60 mins

Son Toni
Crestatx

Platja de Muro

40km, 1¼ hrs

9 S'Albufera ★

Black Vulture
Conservation Foundation
(BVCF)

Caimari

Campanet 11

10

12 Sa Pobla

Can Picafort
p. 82

Moscari

Selva

Búger

21km, 60 mins

Son
Bauló

Mancor
de la Vall

Ma-13

6
San
Real

Biniamar

Inca

Muro
p. 84

Ma-12

Llubí

Santa
Margalida

56km, 60 mins

ESPAÑA

Maria de la Salut

Sencelles

Costitx

Ariany

Cas Canar

Sineu

Ruberts

Lloret de Vistalegre

Petra

MARCO POLO HIGHLIGHTS

★ **CAPDEPERA**
A castle out of a picture book. Imagine the battle cries ringing out from the old towers, walls and battlements, as the pirates lay siege ➤ p. 79

★ **ES ARENAL**
Swim, search for seashells and take a stroll without the hustle and bustle: the protected dune beach near Son Serra de Marina is still surprisingly tranquil ➤ p. 83

★ **S'ALBUFERA**
Discover Mallorca's primeval landscape on a bike ride through the nature park's wetlands of reeds and orchids – an ideal bird habitat ➤ p. 84

★ **LA VICTORIA PENINSULA**
Pretty towns with villas, romantic coves and a hike to Penja Rotja for dream views ➤ p. 89

★ **FORMENTOR PENINSULA**
Panoramic views and sunset at the foot of Talaia d'Albercutx ➤ p. 92

★ **SANTUARI DE LLUC**
Mighty ruins, rugged cliffs and the smell of eucalyptus at Mallorca's most important pilgrimage site ➤ p. 93

CALA RAJADA

(□□ Q5) **Cala Rajada's idyllic port and its fishermen have managed to weather the tourist boom that the largest resort in the northeast has been experiencing since the 1960s.**

This town with its beautiful sea promenade has just 6,800 inhabitants, but in high season they are joined by up to 14,000 tourists.

SIGHTSEEING

SA TORRE CEGA

Following a devastating storm, the gardens, a paradise covering 60,000m² above the port, were closed for nine years. Fortunately, the sculptures, gardens and the exhibition inside the manor house belonging to the March family have now been re-opened to visitors. | *guided tours only (must be pre-booked) March–Nov, Wed, Fri and Sat 11am and 12.30pm, or by arrangement* | *tel. 6 89 02 73 53 or promocio@ajcapdepera.net* | *admission 4.50 euros* | *C/ Juan March 2* | *fundacionbmarch.es* | ⏱ *1½–2 hrs*

EATING & DRINKING

INSIDER TIP
Local fish suppers

Seafood fans flock to Cala Rajada's harbour where there are great fish restaurants supplied daily by the local fishermen, e.g. *Ses Ancores (Thu–Tue 12–3.30pm and daily 6–11pm* | *C/ Leonor Servera 83* | *tel. 9 71 56 58 48* | *€€–€€€)* or *Oleo's (Tue–Sun 12–3.30pm and 6.30–11pm* | *Via Mallorca 2* | *tel. 9 71 56 47 15* | *FB: tonymolipe* | *€€–€€€)*. Make sure to double check prices before ordering as fresh fish can be very expensive.

BEACHES

Cala Rajada, "the bay of rays", is actually made up of a series of small rocky bays which together form one larger bay. *Cala Agulla* is long and benefits from very soft sand. The beach at *Son Moll* is usually extremely crowded in summer, while *Cala de Sa Font* is one for sports fans. 🦅 *Cala Gat* is small and pretty as a picture – a tiny rocky cove surrounded by tall pine trees (great if you need a shady spot). There is an easy 6-km walk along the coast from Cala Gat to Cala Agulla. It goes past the port and the lighthouse, from which (on a clear day) you will be rewarded with a view of Menorca. *Cala*

Mesquida, just as beautiful as Cala Agulla, has a rim of lovely pine trees, but is 10km further up the coast.

The largest club in Cala Rajada is the centrally located *Bolero*. Trendier options are the *Chocolate* open-air bar, the *Physical* club and the *Casa Nova* bar, a local institution which attracts its fair share of VIP visitors.

AROUND CALA RAJADA

1 CAPDEPERA ★

3km from Cala Rajada, 10 mins by car
This little town (pop. 11,400) is crowned by a *castle (daily 10am–8pm,*

Nov–March 10am–5pm | admission 3 euros, in July/Aug 8 euros including concert ticket | capdeperacastell.com | ⏱ 1½–2 hrs), the best-preserved and largest on the island. In the 14th century, the sturdy defensive walls (walkable) enclosed the entirety of Capdepera as it then was: a church, town houses and soldiers' barracks. On a clear day, you can see the island of Menorca, 75km away. ▯ Q5

2 CANYAMEL

8km from Cala Rajada, 10 mins by car
This small holiday resort to the south of Cala Rajada has a long, sandy beach and a reed-lined lagoon. The 18-hole links belonging to the *Canyamel Golf Club (green fee 83–105 euros | tel. 9 71 84 13 13 | canyamel golf.com)* ranks among the more difficult courses on Mallorca. The rustic restaurant *Porxada de Sa Torre (Tue–Sun*

The beautiful beach at Cala Agulla will entice you into the sea

1–3.30pm and daily 7–11pm; closed mid-Nov–end of Feb | tel. 9 71 84 13 10 | torredecanyamel.com | €€), in a medieval fortified tower on the road to Artà, is well-known for its wonderful suckling pig. ⌐ Q6

🖪 COVES D'ARTÀ
11km from Cala Rajada, 15 mins by car

The soot-blackened, chasm-like entrance to these imposing caves is located above the sea near Canyamel – like something out of a fairy tale. *April–June, Oct 10am–6pm; July–Sept 10am–7pm; winter 10am–5pm | 40-min guided tours, admission 15 euros | cuevasdearta.com | ⌐ Q6*

ARTÀ

(⌐ P5) **This small rural town (pop. 7,550) in the furthest reaches of the northeast is crowned by a foreboding citadel, within which lies Sant Salvador, a church that still attracts pilgrims.**

A bit further down, the terraced village is dominated by the equally fortress-like parish church, which was originally built when the island was under Arabic occupation. Cypresses and almond trees dot the ochre of the walls with green. In terms of scenery, expect a few fortified manor houses, flowering gardens and small squares, many bars and a few restaurants. Old traditions, such as raffia and basket weaving, as well as the devil-dancing festivals dedicated to Sant Antoni, are still observed here. The weekly market is held on a Tuesday.

SIGHTSEEING

SANT SALVADOR

From the parish church, there is a cypress-lined path which takes you up to the citadel with depictions of the Stations of the Cross *(Calvario)* accompanying you. Under King Jaume I the Moorish *almudaina* (fortified palace) was turned into a bulwark of Christianity. Inside the church of Sant Salvador, the painting on the right-hand side illustrates the handing over of Mallorca to the Christian king by the Arab Wali. Legends surround the locally revered 17th-century image of the Madonna, telling of how she repeatedly saved the town from pirate attack. Don't forget to take in the view of the harmonious semicircle formed by the town. *Daily 10am–6pm*

CASA DE CULTURA DE NA BATLESA

This "house of culture" is now home to an informative exhibition on Miguel Barceló – the major local contemporary artist. *Mon–Fri 4–7.30pm | free admission | C/ de Ciutat 1*

SES PAÏSSES

This Talaiotic settlement is one of the best maintained and preserved on the island. From 1300 BCE to Roman domination in the first century BCE, it was inhabited by around 300 people. The main entrance and the exterior wall built from heavy megalithic blocks will not fail to impress. The centrally positioned *talaia* (watchtower) is said to

Is it the view or the steps that take your breath away at Artà's citadel?

have been the abode of the chiefs; a good English-language brochure is available. *Signposted* | ⏱ *1–1½ hrs*

EATING & DRINKING

HOTEL SANT SALVADOR

This grand town house in the upper part of town serves light Mediterranean dishes in its three restaurants, all of whose design cleverly melds the classical with the contemporary. Occasional live concerts. *C/ del Pou Nou 26* | *tel. 9 71 82 95 55* | *santsalvador.com* | *€€€*

SHOPPING

Artà's main shopping street, the pedestrianised *Carrer Antoni Blanes*, is great for browsing places offering Mallorcan delicacies, crafts and art.

Can Pantalí (no. 21) is the only shop to still sell baskets made in Artà.

AROUND ARTÀ

🟦 CALA TORTA/CALA MITJANA
10km from Artà, 20 mins by car
A narrow tarmac road takes you to the pretty beaches of 🏖 *Cala Torta* and *Cala Mitjana*. The turn-off is signposted just outside Artà on the way to Capdepera. Although it gets you most of the way there, you will have to walk the final kilometre. To make up for this, there is a beach bar on Cala Torta and occasionally even a bit of surf for the thrill seekers. ᗕ *Q4*

Soak up the sun or cool off in the sea at Cala Mitjana

5 ERMITA DE BETLEM
9.5km from Artà, 25 mins by car

Those who brave the hairpin bends across the rather barren *Puig de Sa Font Crutia* may well think this hermitage and its gardens are a mirage at first sight. It is set in a fertile valley, high up in the hills which has been cultivated since the Moorish period. There were once more than 30 farms all around the retreat, which was founded in 1805 (and christened *Betlem*, or Bethlehem). The last monks moved to their order's headquarters in Palma in 2010, but you may still visit the chapel with its avenue of cypresses, and the *mirador* with sweeping views across the bay of Alcúdia. The nearby holy well of *Sa Font* makes an idyllic place for a picnic. *The road begins at Artà Castle | ☉ 1 hr | ⬚ O4*

CAN PICAFORT

(⬚ M–N4) **In summer, the rather faceless resort of Can Picafort (pop. 7,300), with its many bars and shops and a 5-km sandy beach, becomes fairly lively.**

The eastern beach of *Son Bauló* marks the beginning of a coastal conservation area.

EATING & DRINKING

ES MOLINO
On simple wooden chairs under pine trees you can munch the best beautifully tender barbecued rabbit on the island. *Tue–Sun 9am–2am | C/ Badía 4 | tel. 9 71 85 02 49 | €*

MELASSA

A restaurant whose décor and ambience feels as authentic as the tasty seafood it serves. *Daily 8–10.30am and 6.30–10.30pm | tel. 9 71 85 08 51 | C/ Isabel Garau 49 | melassa.es | €€*

SPORT & ACTIVITIES

Guided horse treks can be booked through *Rancho Grande (25 euros/ hr | exit Ctra. Alcúdia–Artà, at Km21.5| ranchocanpi cafort.com).*

The local *go-karting track (May– Oct daily 10am–10pm; Nov–April Tue–Sun 9am–1pm and 3–7pm | 10 mins from 15 euros | Ctra. Alcudia– Artà s/n | Santa Margarita | kartingcanpicafort.com)* allows children to feel the wind in their hair (in tandem karts where their parents actually put the pedal to the metal).

AROUND CAN PICAFORT

6 SON REAL

6km from Can Picafort, 10 mins by car
This stately home was bought by the Balearic government in 2004. It contains a well-curated museum of life on the island in the 19th and 20th centuries as well as a short film on the finca itself. It is also a good starting point for a scramble through the undergrowth down to the impressive *Son Real Necropolis* on the sea's edge. This huge cemetery was in use between around 700 and 200BCE. There were once as many as 2,000 graves here,

INSIDER TIP
City of the dead

built using large stones. Excavations have been going on for some years and in 2018, around 300 skeletons (alongside a treasure trove of grave goods) were removed and are now on display in Barcelona. *Daily 9am–4pm | free admission | exit the Ma12 at Km17.7 | ⏱ 3 hrs*

7 SON SERRA DE MARINA

8km from Can Picafort, 10 mins by car
This new Wild West-themed holiday resort (pop. 700) has lots of beach bars and restaurants with terraces. Beyond it, the little-frequented protected dune beach of ★ *Es Arenal* stretches for some 2.5km to Colònia de Sant Pere; there are no deckchairs or parasols available. At the very end of the beach nudism is tolerated. A *talaiot* marks the access road at Km14.2 on the road leading to Artà. ▥ *N5*

8 COLÒNIA DE SANT PERE

20km from Can Picafort, 25 mins by car
This sleepy-looking village (pop. 550) on the eastern end of Alcúdia Bay makes a good destination for long beach walks from Can Picafort, or the starting point for hikes on the Ferrutx peninsula. The town has a pretty boulevard along the sea front lined by a few bars and restaurants. The restaurant and bar *Sa Xarxa (Tue–Sun noon–11pm | Paseo del Mar s/n | tel. 9 71 58 92 51 | sa-xarxa.com | €€)*, located at one end, serves an eclectic

selection of dishes with influences from all over the world. ◫ 04

MURO

(◫ L4–5) **The agricultural town of Muro (pop. 6,800) is one of the oldest settlements on the island, having received town status as early as 1300.**

The huge church – whose belltower (once a defence fortification) is only connected to the nave via a small bridge – is as impressive as the stately old townhouses in the *Comtat* part of town. The people of Muro are some of the least used to tourists on the island – even the Sunday market does not bring many tourists in.

SIGHTSEEING

MUSEU ETNOLÒGIC DE MURO 🐖
The ethnological museum housed in a 17th-century townhouse holds an exhibition on rural life in the olden days with exhibits on traditional crafts and everyday life back in the day. *Sept–July Tue–Sat 10am–3pm, Thu also 5–8pm, closed in Aug | free admission | C/ Major 15 | ⟳ 2 hrs*

EATING & DRINKING

SA FONDA
A large bar, a small dining room, a barbecue and an open fireplace in the winter provide the simple setting for solid home-made fare. *Mon, Wed, Thu 6.30am–8pm, Fri–Sun to midnight,*

Tue closed. | C/ Sant Jaume 1 | tel. 9 71 53 79 65 | €

AROUND MURO

🟦 S'ALBUFERA ⭐ 🐖
10km from Muro, 10 mins by car
Covering 17km², this natural park northeast of Muro is teeming with wildlife. More than 10,000 migratory birds pass through; there are also amphibians, wild horses and orchids. The flat terrain is best explored by bike; rental bikes are available in Port d'Alcúdia or Pollença, e.g. at *Sport Bequi (tel. 9 71 54 56 64 | sportbequi. com)* or *New Horizon (tel. 9 71 59 79 87 | newhorizon.es)*. Don't forget your binoculars! Information at the *Centre Recepció* in the park *(tel. 9 71 89 22 50). April–Sept 9am–6pm; Oct–March 9am–5pm | Ctra. Alcúdia-Can Picafort | Entrance on the Pont dels Anglesos | ⟳ 2½–3 hrs | ◫ L-M 3-4*

🟦 BLACK VULTURE CONSERVATION FOUNDATION (BVCF)
11km from Muro, 15 mins by bar
A chance to get up close and personal with black vultures – the birds that symbolise Mallorca. These imposing scavengers (with a wingspan of up to 3m) can normally only be seen circling high in the sky above the Tramuntana mountains. The woody Son Pons Finca, which serves as a sanctuary for injured birds, offers an opportunity to see

them at a proximity that would simply be impossible in the wild. Try to be there at feeding time when the vultures are most active. There is also an excellent exhibition and a short film on the birds and their habitat. *Mon, Fri and the first Sat in the month June–Aug 9am–1pm, Sept–May 10am–2pm | free admission | Finca Son Pons | Take exit 35 on the Palma–Alcúdia motorway | bvcf.eu | ⏱ 1½ hrs | ⎕ K4*

🔟 CAMPANET

14km from Muro, 10 mins by car

This sparsely populated quiet village comes alive twice a week for its market on Tuesdays and Saturdays. On these days young and old rub shoulders at the tapas counter in *Sa Galerie* bar. Traditional crafts such as glass-blowing, basket-weaving and pottery have survived here. Buy glass directly from the producers at *Menestralía*'s factory *(exit 35 of the Palma–Alcúdia motorway)*. Also worth seeing are the superb stalactite and stalagmite formations at the ⛪ *Coves de Campanet (daily May–Oct 10am–6.30pm; Nov–April 10am–5.30pm | admission 15 euros | near exit 37 | covesdecampanet.com | ⏱ tour 40 mins). ⎕ K4*

1️⃣2️⃣ SA POBLA

5km from Muro, 10 mins by car

While this farming village (pop. 12,700) might not be pretty, it is Mallorca's agricultural heart and has preserved some characteristics that have died out elsewhere. Traditional festivals such as Sant Antoni are still celebrated, and there is a rural Sunday market fringed with tapas bars

Spot egrets and more in the S'Albufera natural park

offering spicy regional dishes. On hot August nights, while much of the island holds chill-out sessions and beach parties, hundreds of music lovers descend on the market square for the *Jazz Festival sa Pobla (jazz.sapobla.cat)* to listen to bands from all over the world. ⎕ L4

INSIDER TIP Let's swing!

ALCÚDIA

(⎕ M2–3) **Some say the difference between Alcúdia and its port (total pop. 19,400), a mile or so away, is like that between heaven and hell.**

The *Port d'Alcúdia*, represents the nadir of the tourist boom on the island with its 30,000 hotel beds housed in

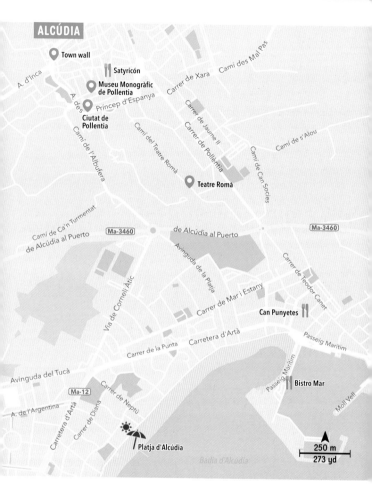

bland buildings which stretch from the harbour to the Platja de Muro. In summer, British, Scandinavian and German tourists throng the streets, and youngsters fill the pubs and clubs every night.

Compared to this, the small town of Alcúdia seems to have a near dream-like quality: cars are banned from the town centre, which allows for carefree strolling, and a large number of restaurant terraces decked out in flowers beckon guests. Prettily decorated little shops invite some serious browsing.

SIGHTSEEING

TOWN WALL

In 1298 under King Jaume II, work started on the town wall as a defence against pirate raids. By 1660, several bulwarks and a second ring of walls had been added to further bolster the defences. The parish church of *Sant Jaume (May–Oct Mon–Sat 10am–1pm; for Mass Tue–Fri 8.30pm, Sat 7pm, Sun 12.30pm, 7.30pm; Nov–April only open for Mass Tue, Wed, Fri, Sat 7.30pm, Sun 9.30am, 12pm and 7.30pm | admission 1 euro)* – with its pretty 14th-century rose window – is built into the wall. It was mainly built in the 16th and 19th centuries. Inside, visitors will find a magnificent high altar with a statue of Saint James. The small side chapel, in Renaissance style, has a wooden *Santcrist* crucifix which is shown every three years at the procession for the feast of Santa Ana.

MUSEU MONOGRÀFIC DE POLLENTIA

The model of a Roman house helps to create a picture of what Pollentia used to be like. The museum houses finds from the Talaiotic and Roman eras and other important archaeological pieces from Pollentia. *Mon–Fri 9.30am–8.30pm, Sat/Sun 9.30am–2.30pm; Oct–March Mon–Fri 9.30am–3.30pm | admission see Ciutat de Pollentia | C/ Sant Jaume 30 | ⊙ 1½–2 hrs*

CIUTAT DE POLLENTIA

Pollentia is the main site for Roman finds on the island. In 123 BCE, the Balearic Islands were conquered by the Roman consul Caecilius Metellius, and around 50 years later, in 70 BCE, Pollentia was founded to become the capital of Mallorca. In 426 CE, Pollentia was destroyed by the Vandals. The new town that rose from its ruins a little further north, under Muslim rule, was Alcúdia. Today, all that is left to see are a few columns and the foundation walls of the *Casa de la Portella. Mon–Fri 9.30am–8.30pm, Sat/Sun 9.30am–2.30pm | admission 4 euros incl. Museu Monogràfic | Av. Prínceps d'Espanya | ⊙ 1 hr*

TEATRE ROMÀ 🐾

Like its larger counterparts, Spain's smallest amphitheatre has retained its foundation walls and its semicircular staircase. It once had a capacity of 20,000. The tiered seating sits on top of prehistoric caves, and at the entrance there are some trapezium-shaped tombs dating back to the sixth century. *Mon–Fri 9.30am–2.30pm | admission free | Port d'Alcúdia, 200m along path from Ctra. Alcúdia | ⊙ 1 hr*

EATING & DRINKING

BISTRO MAR

As you relish the tasty fish and meat dishes served in this well-kept bistro you can enjoy the view of the smart yachts and the sea from the patio. *Daily 12–9pm; closed Nov–March | Passeig Marítim 3 | Port d'Alcúdia | tel. 9 71 54 57 04 | bistromar.com | €€*

CAN PUNYETES

Andalusian watering hole in Port d'Alcúdia, small and always packed, serving a huge choice of the best tapas. *Wed–Mon 12.30–4.30pm and 6pm–midnight; closed mid-Nov–end Feb | C/ Barques 1 | Port d'Alcúdia | tel. 9 71 54 83 52 | €*

SATYRICÓN

In the lavishly restored former cinema of *Alcúdia* (note the fabulous ceiling fresco), you can experience the joys of ancient Roman culinary culture. *Daily 10am–11pm; closed Nov–March | Plaça Constitució 4 | tel. 9 71 54 49 97 | €€*

SHOPPING

The Carrer Major contains many small shops and boutiques. *Àgata (no. 48)* stocks a wealth of rocks and minerals. *Oska (no. 34a)* is a fashion boutique. *Sa Cisterna* at the corner of the eponymous side street offers a well-stocked wine bodega *(closed Thu)* and Mallorcan delicacies. *Torrons Vicens (C/ del Moll 3b)* is nougat heaven.

SPORT & ACTIVITIES

The bays of Pollença and Alcúdia have good sailing, stand-up paddleboarding and windsurfing areas, and are suitable for beginners too. The sweeping sandy beach of *Platja d'Alcúdiais* is ideal for children, as it remains shallow far into the sea, allowing for plenty of paddling.

CLUB DE GOLF ALCANADA

The island's prettiest golf course: 16 of the 18 holes boast sea views; the clubhouse has a good restaurant and a panoramic terrace. *Green fees from 105 euros | Ctra. del Faro | Port d'Alcúdia | tel. 9 71 54 95 60*

HIDROPARK

Need a quick shot of adrenalin? Then get yourself to Port d'Alcúdia's waterpark. Corkscrew slides, ramps made from tyres, wave pools, chill-out zones and a children's paddling pool await you. *May–June and Sept–Oct daily 10am–5pm; July–Aug daily 10am–6pm | adults 24.90 euros, children 3–11 17.90 euros | Av. Tucà | Port d'Alcúdia | hidroparkalcudia.com*

After a strenuous day at the beach, refuel in one of Alcúdia's appealing restaurants

WIND & FRIENDS WATERSPORTS
Sailing and windsurfing school on the beach belonging to the Hotel Sunwing Alcudia Beach. *5-day sailing course 260 euros, 5-day windsurfing course 240 euros | 15 April–end Oct | Port d'Alcúdia | tel. 6 61 74 54 14 | windfriends.com |*

NIGHTLIFE

The *Auditorio (tel. 9 71 89 71 85)* opposite the town wall hosts theatre performances and concerts from pop to classical (programme can be found online and in local press).

The most popular clubs are *Menta (Av. Tucà 5 | menta-disco.com)* and *Magic (near the Burger King roundabout);* both are in Port d' d'Alcúdia.

AROUND ALCÚDIA

🔟 MUSEO SA BASSA BLANCA – FUNDACIÓN YANNICK Y BEN JAKOBER
7km from Alcúdia, 15 mins by car
This gallery has a stunningly beautiful setting. Its collection is made up of works by Yannick and Ben Jakober and an unusual collection of historical portraits of children from the 16th–18th centuries. There are also guided tours of the grand house next door. Don't miss out on a visit to the rose garden, which makes up a considerable part

INSIDER TIP
Bloomin' wonderful

of the property and has more than 100 English rose varieties. Beautiful all year round, in May the gardens bursts into vibrant bloom. *Mon–Sat 10am–6pm | admission 10 euros, garden alone 5 euros | 🐾 free admission Tue 2–6pm | Camino de Ronda 10 | Mal Pas | fundacionjakober.org | ⏱ 2–3 hrs*

🔟 LA VICTORIA PENINSULA ⭐
6km from Alcúdia, 15 mins by car
The road from Alcúdia (well signposted) leads past the pretty villas of *Mal Pas* and *Bonaire* – with their marinas – before winding around a series of small romantic bays and heading up to the *Ermita de la Victoria*. The locals revere the *Virgen de la Victoria*, a Gothic figure often compared to the Virgin Mary and patron saint of Alcúdia, who according to legend once saved the town from pirates. Dating from 1679, the church looks like a fortress. Next to the church, *Mirador (Tue–Sun 1–3.30pm and 7pm–midnight | tel. 9 71 54 71 73 | miradordelavictoria.com | €€)* mainly caters to day-trippers who flock to its terrace for the sensational views of Pollença bay.

Along the way to the *Ermita de la Victoria* a perfectly laid-out picnic site provides an inviting location by the sea. From the Ermita, the hike along the high cliffs up to Penja Rotja

INSIDER TIP
Don't look down

is well worth doing for the superb views across the bay of Pollença, and only takes about 45 minutes. The path is signposted but does at one point require a head for heights. *▥ M–N 2–3*

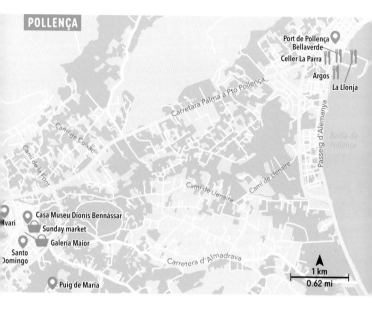

POLLENÇA

(⊞ K–L2) **The wealthy rural town (pop. 16,200) in the far north of the island is one of a kind.**

The Pollençins maintain their own dialect and the practice of traditional crafts. In general, it is an arty place, with a dozen art galleries as and an annual international music festival. Pollença definitely stands out from the rest of the provincial towns on the island.

SIGHTSEEING

CALVARI

The 365 steps following the Stations of the Cross lead to a small church popular with pilgrims and with a great view. *Behind the market square, past the Rooster Fountain (signposted)*

CASA MUSEU DIONÍS BENNÀSSAR

The painter Dionís Bennàssar (1904–67) belonged to the group around the Art Nouveau painter Hermenegildo Anglada Camarasa. His former home is today run as a museum, showing 240 of his best works. *Mar–Oct Tue–Sat 10.30am–2pm and 5–8pm, Sun 10.30am–2pm, or by appointment | C/ Roca 14 | tel. 9 71 53 09 97 | museu dionisbennassar.com | ⊙ 1–1½ hrs*

SANTO DOMINGO

In August, the courtyard (with beautiful cloisters) of the former Dominican monastery (now an old people's home) hosts an international music festival *(festivalpollenca.com)*. On winter Sundays, Mallorcan folklore takes over.

The *Museu Municipal* is also housed here, and has an excellent exhibition on local history, including finds from the Talaiotic period, and a picture gallery. *Tue–Sat 10am–1pm, May–Oct also 5.30–8.30pm | 🐷 admission free | ⊙ 1 hr*

PUIG DE MARIA

The best way to get to the town's local "mountain" (333m), which is crowned by the former convent of *Mare de Déu del Puig*, is to park your car when you reach the last houses in the town. From here, walk first on the road, then on an ancient pilgrims' path. Your reward will be a stunning view and a pit stop at the convent's refectory. *Ctra. Palma–Pollença at Km51*

PORT DE POLLENÇA

Stretching out west from the fishing port and marina of Pollença Bay, the island's most beautiful pedestrian promenade runs under ancient pines and is flanked by pretty villas and hotels from the early 20th century.

EATING & DRINKING

ARGOS

Young, talented and pretty inventive, Alvaro Salazar runs the stove at Argos in the Hotel La Goleta. His modern Mediterranean food has been rewarded with a Michelin star. Both the food and the sea views are stunning. *Wed–Mon 7–9.30pm | Paseo Saralegui 118 | Port de Pollença | tel. 9 71 86 59 02 | argosrestaurant.com | €€–€€€*

BELLAVERDE

It does not get much greener than the restaurant of Pension Bellavista: the divine gardens of the Bellaverde and their ancient fig trees provide just the right setting for the creative vegan and vegetarian menu. *Tue–Sun 8.30am–midnight | C/ de les Monges 14 | Port de Pollença | tel. 6 75 60 25 28 | FB: RestauranteBellaverde | €€*

CELLER LA PARRA

Over-the-top decoration, but authentic island cuisine and very cosy. Excellent paella served to you while you sit among huge bulging casks of wine. *Tue–Sun 1–3.30pm and 7–10.30pm | C/ Joan XXIII 84 | Port de Pollença | tel. 9 71 86 50 41 | cellerlaparra.com | €€*

INSIDER TIP
Try a super traditional paella

LA LLONJA

The old fish market has been turned into one of the best gourmet restaurants in the north, with a beautiful view of the harbour from upstairs on the terrace and a sunny bistro below. *Daily 12.30–4pm and 7.30–11pm; closed Nov–mid-Dec | Moll Vell | tel. 9 71 86 84 30 | restaurantlallonja.com | €€–€€€*

SHOPPING

GALERÍA MAIOR

The most avant-garde of the local galleries has an extensive repertoire of international artists. *Plaça Major 4 | galeriamaior.es*

SUNDAY MARKET

On Sunday mornings in the large market square you can buy fruit and vegetables, regional products and crafts, and honey from Artà at the stall *Mel de na Marta*. Around the square there are great bars, such as *Can Moixet (daily from 7am)*.

SPORT & ACTIVITIES

GOLF POLLENÇA

Nine-hole golf links, with lovely far-reaching views from the clubhouse (which has its own swimming pool and restaurant). *Green fees from 45 euros | exit Ctra. Palma–Pollença at Km49 | tel. 9 71 53 32 16 | golf pollensa.com*

SAIL & SURF

Mallorca's largest sailing and wind-surfing school also offers boat hire. *Passeig Saralegui 134 | tel. 9 71 86 53 46 | www.sailsurf.de/en*

AROUND POLLENÇA

15 FORMENTOR PENINSULA ★

23km from Pollença, 35 mins by car

This long, narrow peninsula and its sheer cliffs has attracted up to 7,000 cars a day in peak season. As a result, the main access road has now been closed to most drivers in July and August (10am–7pm). Instead, there are shuttle buses to get you to the cape itself ⚑ *(from Port de Pollença | single fare 1.55 euros)*. During the rest of the year, you need to get there early in the morning or in the early evening

to avoid huge traffic jams on the picturesque 18-km-long road.

Perhaps of more interest than the cape itself is the *mirador* on the last stretch of road before the peninsula, where you get great views of the photogenic rocky islet of *Es Colomer*, and its sheer 200-m-high rock faces, as well as the pirate tower of *Talaia d'Albercutx*. The ascent takes around half an hour and you'll be rewarded with panoramic views across half the island and a spectacular sunset.

Time for the beach? *Cala Pi* is pretty but small and often crowded. More secluded are the two natural bays of *Cala Figuera* and *Cala Murta*, which can only be reached on foot. 🚧 *M–N 1–2*

16 CALA SANT VICENÇ

7km from Pollença, 15 mins by car

This small villa-lined resort northeast of Port de Pollença can easily be reached by bike. There are several bike-hire options in Pollença, including *Rent March (rentmarch.com)* in the port. The two soft sandy bays are set against the mountain backdrop of the *Cavall Bernat* whose sheer rock face rises up from the sea. The mountain massif turns different colours depending on the season and the position of the sun.

INSIDER TIP
Magic mountain

In the afternoons in February and March, the shadow on the rock assumes the shape of a horse and rider: an image that has inspired countless painters and photographers.

The *Cala Sant Vicenç* hotel has an excellent restaurant, the *Lavanda (daily 10.30am–11pm; closed*

The sanctuary church of Lluc houses the highly revered statue of the *Moreneta*

mid-Oct–April | tel. 9 71 53 02 50 | €€–€€€), a great place for lunch or for a refreshing G&T in the evening. *Cala Barques (daily 12.30–3.30pm and Tue–Sat 7.30–10.15pm; closed Oct–early Jan | tel. 9 71 53 06 91 | €€)* has a veranda with amazing views, and serves excellent fish. ▱ *L1*

⓱ SANTUARI DE LLUC ★

20km from Pollença, 30 mins by car

Against an imposing mountain backdrop of sheer rock faces and amid fragrant eucalyptus trees, Mallorca's most important pilgrimage site sits in a valley at 525m above sea level. Coachloads of visitors make their way to the *Moreneta*, the Black Madonna in the monastery church. Picnic areas line the monastic complex which was built in the 17th and 18th centuries. Legend has it that in the 14th century a shepherd boy found the statue of the Virgin Mary and took it to the priest at Escorca three times. Every time, the Madonna returned to the place where she had been found, indicating her choice for the spot where a hermitage should be built. You can spend the night in the Santuari's old cells *(€)*. Amazingly, they are en suite!

> **INSIDER TIP**
> It's a monk's life

The *blavets*, choir boys, have been singing at Mass here since the 16th century *(Mass Mon–Sat 12.45pm, Sun 11am | 5 euros incl. museum, film, garden, plunge pool in summer, parking | tel. 9 71 87 15 25 | lluc.net | ⏱ 1½–2 hrs)*. The cosy mountain restaurant *Es Guix (Wed–Mon 12.30–4pm, check website for winter hours | 2km from Lluc on the way towards Sóller | tel. 9 71 51 70 92| esguix.com | €€)* has a mountain rock pool fed by spring water and serves Mallorcan cuisine. ▱ *J3*

THE EAST

IMPOSSIBLY IDYLLIC

With its white sand, pine-fringed beaches, turquoise sea and whitewashed houses, the east coast is Mallorca's most cheerful side.

This coast would be a Mediterranean idyll if it weren't for the fact that far too many holidaymakers come here in high season. The small bays are unable to cope with the sheer number of visitors or the thousands of yachts and gin palaces that crowd their waters. Apart from Cala Millor/Sa Coma, parts of the Cales de Mallorca and Portocristo

Fishing boats still bob in the harbour at Portocolom

Novo, the strip of coast between Cap d'es Pins and the Punta de Sa Galera has been constructed in comparatively good taste.

One of the island's most beautiful drives, the Ma4014, runs between the coast and the Serra de Llevant mountain range. Here almond plantations, gardens with apricot and orange trees, arable fields and vineyards accompany cyclists and drivers on their tour through the gentle landscape. Countless beaches are accessible by leaving the Ma4014 to take little roads to the sea.

THE EAST

Sant Joan

Petra

Vilafranca
de Bonany

Ma-15

Manacor p. 101

ESPAÑA

14km, 20 mins

13km, 30 mins

Son Macià

Felanitx

1 Puig de Sant Salvador ★

5 Castell de Santueri

es Carritxó

Cas Concos **6**

s'Horta

Cala Sa Nau **4**

s'Alqueria Blanca

Cala Ferrera

Cala d'Or

3 km
1.86 mi

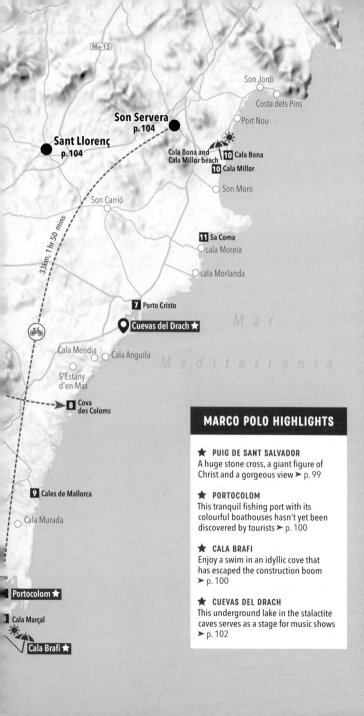

Ma-15

Son Jordi

Costa dels Pins

Port Nou

Son Servera
p. 104

Sant Llorenç
p. 104

Cala Bona and
Cala Millor beach **10** Cala Bona
10 Cala Millor

Son Moro

Son Carrió

33km, 1 hr 50 mins

11 Sa Coma
cala Moreia

cala Morlanda

7 Porto Cristo

Cuevas del Drach ★

Mar

Cala Mendia   Cala Anguila

S'Estany
d'en Mas

Mediterrània

8 Cova
des Coloms

9 Cales de Mallorca

Cala Murada

Portocolom ★

Cala Marçal

Cala Brafi ★

MARCO POLO HIGHLIGHTS

★ **PUIG DE SANT SALVADOR**
A huge stone cross, a giant figure of
Christ and a gorgeous view ➤ p. 99

★ **PORTOCOLOM**
This tranquil fishing port with its
colourful boathouses hasn't yet been
discovered by tourists ➤ p. 100

★ **CALA BRAFI**
Enjoy a swim in an idyllic cove that
has escaped the construction boom
➤ p. 100

★ **CUEVAS DEL DRACH**
This underground lake in the stalactite
caves serves as a stage for music shows
➤ p. 102

FELANITX

(□□ M–N9) **At first glance you wouldn't think that the sleepy rural town of Felanitx had 17,300 inhabitants – except on a Sunday when the weekly market breathes life into the area around Plaça Espanya, the historic and scenic centre.**

In the Moorish period, Felanitx was at the forefront of the *azulejo* (blue tile) industry. Nowadays, the town survives through a mix of tourism, cultivating fruit, producing wine, farming cattle, fishing, and various other small businesses. The former role of Felanitx as a centre of agriculture is evident, and a few of the original 25 mill towers are still standing. In 1957 Felanitx saw the birth of Miquel Barceló, arguably Mallorca's most important contemporary painter. His works mostly represent nature and one of his paintings is on display in Palma's cathedral.

SIGHTSEEING

SANT MIQUEL PARISH CHURCH

Rising above an imposing flight of steps, the 18th-century church boasts a magnificent rose window and an ornately decorated portal.

CALVARI

Atop the Calavari with its simple, 19th-century chapel *(usually closed)*, the view of the town is quite spectacular. Starting from the church, turn down Carrer Major and then right onto Carrer d'es Call to get to the steps marking the beginning of the Way of the Cross.

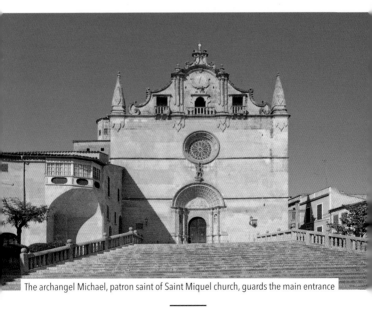

The archangel Michael, patron saint of Saint Miquel church, guards the main entrance

EATING & DRINKING

CAFÉ D'ES MERCAT

This simple café opposite the covered market is always buzzing thanks to its relaxed atmosphere and the incredible value of their lunch menus. For 9 euros you get food, water, wine and even coffee. *Sun–Fri 6am–4pm | C/Major 26 | tel. 9 71 58 00 08 | €*

INSIDER TIP
Lunch on a budget

EL CASTILLO DEL BOSQUE

The castle-like décor may be a matter of taste, but the Mediterranean menu featuring Mallorcan dishes is entirely recommendable and a favourite among visitors from mainland Spain. *Thu–Tue 1–3.30pm and 7–10.30pm | on the road towards Portocolom, at Km8 | large but busy car park | tel. 9 71 82 41 44 | elcastillodelbosque.es | €€*

ESTRAGON

Inexpensive, but good, this small terrace restaurant right in the heart of Felanitx scores high with a good-value and tasty daily set menu for 12 euros. À la carte, you can order monkfish, duck, lamb shoulder and more. *Wed–Sun 7–11pm, Sat/Sun also 1–3pm | Plaça Perelada 14 | tel. 9 71 58 33 03 | estragon-felanitx.com | €–€€*

SHOPPING

You shouldn't return home from Felanitx without some sort of earthenware souvenir. These can be found at, for example, *Cerámiques Mallorca (Mon–Fri 10.30am–7.30pm | C/ de Sant Agustí 50)* or *Call Vermell (Tue–Fri 10am–1pm, 5–8pm, Sun 10am–1pm | C/ Major 44)*, a ceramics workshop with its own shop.

SUNDAY MARKET

From around 10am the heart of the town gets busy with open-air and covered markets. There is hardly standing space in the pubs along the palm-lined *Plaça Espanya*.

SPORT & ACTIVITIES

Country life at its very best. Explore the lovely paths around Felantix on foot or by bike. There are good guides available from all tourist information offices.

AROUND FELANITX

🔟 PUIG DE SANT SALVADOR ⭐

8km from Felanitx, 20 mins by car to Santuario de Sant Salvador

The holy mountain of Felanitx (509m) has a double summit. The higher peak of the two is crowned by an abandoned monastery which has its origins in the 13th century. The complex contains a statue of the Virgin Mary from the same period and a Gothic alabaster altarpiece. An oversized stone cross on the second peak and a huge statue of Christ are reminders of how much power the Church once had here. *▥ N9*

☑ PORTOCOLOM ★

12km from Felanitx, 15 mins by car

The former port of Felanitx has retained its quiet charm and beauty with its well-preserved fishermen's houses and boathouses, as well as many traditional *llaüts* (Mallorcan fishing boats). However, it is set to grow under recent plans.

The number of inhabitants (4,500) triples in high season, when the residents of Felanitx move into their summer houses. Historical research may say otherwise but local legend, has it that Christopher Columbus was born in Portocolom, hence the name.

If you're hungry, *Hostals HPC (kitchen 12.30–4pm and 6.30–11pm, see website for winter opening | C/ Cristófol Colom 5 | tel. 9 71 82 53 23 | hostalportocolom.com | €€)*, on the promenade, is worthy of a visit from when it opens at 9am. Next door, *Colón (Thu–Tue 11am–midnight | C/ Cristófol Colom 7 | tel. 9 71 82 47 83 | restaurante-colon.com |€€€)* serves excellent Mediterranean cuisine in a refined atmosphere with a little hint of the Alps thanks to it well-known Austrian chef Dieter Sögner. *▦ O10*

☑ CALA MARÇAL

10km from Felanitx, 20 mins by car

Portocolom's nearest beach is dominated by a hotel of the same name. Behind Cala Marçal and only accessible on foot, there's the small, charming ★ ⛱ *Cala Brafi*, a beach that has escaped the construction boom. The way to this idyllic cove is to take a "hidden" narrow path running along a wall from the upper part of town behind Cala Marçal. *▦ O10*

Enjoy the bucolic rural landscape around Cas Concos at the edge of the Serra de Levant

4 CALA SA NAU 🏝
12km from Felanitx, 20 mins by car
The relaxed bar *Xiringuito Cala Sa Nau (summer Mon–Sun 9am–the small hours | tel. 6 37 83 32 76 | clasanau. com | €€)* serves delicious hamburgers. The water here is turquoise, there are sunshades, a loo and a car park next door. Put simply, Cala Sa Nau is the perfect beach for a perfect day. 🚗 O10

5 CASTELL DE SANTUERI
8km from Felanitx, 15 mins by car
The ruins of this massive medieval fortification sit on a mountaintop south of Felanitx. It is worth exploring for its panoramic views and the place's bizarre feeling of being far away from everything. The views stretch far across the countryside and the sea. The website has information on the history of the site. *April-Oct Mon-Sat 10.30am-6.30pm, Sun 10.30am–2pm; Nov–March Sat/Sun 10am–2pm and 4–6pm | admission 4 euros | santueri.org | ⏱ 1–1½ hr | 🚗 N10*

6 CAS CONCOS
8km, 15 mins by car
The drive through fields and hills to this village with 420 inhabitants is part of the attraction. Cas Concos itself would not be remarkable if the village and surrounding area didn't offer some great pitstops for hungry tourists. The eternally popular and hip *Viena (Wed–Mon from 6pm | C/ Metge Obrador 13 | tel. 9 71 84 22 90 | €€)* is in new hands following the death of its founder, but they have not changed much (including the menu). A few houses further on (no. 23), a Chilean

family runs the modern *Can Pelat (Thu-Tue 6.30–11pm, closed lunchtime | tel. 9 71 83 96 43 | €€)*, offering imaginative Mediterranean cuisine.

MANACOR

(🚗 N7) **The island's third-largest town gets a fairly bad press in most travel guides. However, the church square with its cafés and bars has kept an authentic feel.**

More than other places, the town centre belongs to its inhabitants. Apart from tourism, Manacor (pop. 41,000) makes a fair living from the souvenir and furniture industry that has settled around the town.

SIGHTSEEING

TORRE DELS ENAGISTES
This fortified tower and palace dates back to the 13th century. Today, it houses the 🐗 *Historical Museum (June-mid-Sept Mon, Wed-Sat 9am–2pm, Thu-Sun 5–8.30pm; mid-Sept–May Mon-Sat 9am-2pm, Thu-Sat 5–7.30pm, Sun 10.30am–1pm | admission free)*, with mosaics and objects from the early Christian basilicas of Son Peretó and Sa Carrotxa at Manacor. The sturdy building alone is worth the visit. *Ctra. Cales de Mallorca, Km1.5*

RAFA NADAL SPORTS CENTRE
Rafa Nadal loves his island and his hometown of Manacor. One could say that he has raised a monument to this love (or to himself) with his sports

centre. The academy has sports facilities, a hotel for students and a merchandise store. The tennis star's trophies and medals are exhibited in the *Museum Xperience (daily 10am–6.30pm | admission 15 euros | Crta. Cales de Mallorca | rnsportscentre.com).*

EATING & DRINKING

CAN MARCH

Enjoy modern Mallorcan cuisine in a cosy and somewhat hidden away family-run restaurant. *Tue–Sun 1–3.30pm | C/ València 7 | tel. 9 71 55 00 02 | canmarch.com | €–€€|*

FACTORIA

A young and fresh gastro bar which markets itself as a factory for food-based thrills.

SHOPPING

CAN GARANYA 40

INSIDER TIP
Browsing at its best

Even if you don't urgently need a new walking stick or a hammock, you have to check out this shop. A huge range of everyday items with practically no plastic in sight. Almost no-one manages to leave without buying some kind of souvenir. Further down the same street (nos. 30 and 51), the same family runs two shoe shops. One sells *aubarcas*, the trendy leather flip-flops, and hand-embroidered espadrilles. The other specialises in slightly smarter shoes and handbags. *Mon–Sat 9.30am–1.30pm and 5–8.30pm | C/ Joan Lliteras 40*

AROUND MANACOR

⑦ PORTO CRISTO

13km from Manacor, 15 mins by car
This small town (pop. 7,350) to the east of Manacor is a pretty place, thanks to its rounded harbour bay and the *torrent*, on which *llaüts* and yachts gently bob. Porto Cristo owes its fame to the largest stalactite caves on the island. The *Coves del Hams (daily 10am–4pm, 4.30pm or 5pm – check the website | admission incl. digital show 21 euros | cuevas-hams.com)* are right at the entrance to the town on the road from Manacor *(well signposted)*. They offer a guided tour, a show set on a small underground lake and a virtual Jules Verne show.

The "Caves of the Dragon" or ★ *Cuevas del Drach (mid-March–Oct daily 10am–5pm on the hour every hour except 1pm, Nov–mid-March 10.45am, 12pm, 2pm and 3.30pm | admission 15.50 euros | Ctra. Cuevas | cuevasdeldrach.com | ☉ 1 hr)* also offer guided tours around this special place where the temperature never changes from 21°C. Here, the largest underground lake in the world is the stage for a kitschy but beautiful tourist spectacle: a boat with a mini-orchestra glides over the lake emerging from complete darkness into the light. Afterwards, visitors can go for a short ride on the boat. The caves are popular, so aim to come early in the morning or later in the afternoon. Access is through the village of Porto Cristo,

Fantastical forms in the Cuevas del Drach

from where you follow the brown signs to the southern end of town.

A culinary delight in Porto Cristo is hidden in a seemingly unspectacular location. *Roland (Mon–Sat 1–3pm and 6.30–10.30pm | C/ Sant Jordi 5 | tel. 9 71 82 01 29 | roland-restaurant.es | €€)* serves excellent gourmet cuisine with a Mallorcan touch (strudel with black pudding 'Botifarrons') and the service is excellent. *P8*

ⓧ COVA DES COLOMS

14km from Manacor, 30 mins by car

The "Cave of Pigeons" – with its fresh-water lake and stunning stalactites and stalagmites – is as large as a cathedral. It sits just below a small headland between the coves of Cala Falcó and Cala Varques and is most easily approached by swimming or by boat. The diving schools *Skualo (tel. 9 71 81 50 94 | www.skualo.com)* in Porto Cristo and Portocolom will take you to explore the cave on a half-day excursion *(69 euros)*. They provide wetsuits and torches.

You can also get to Cova des Coloms on foot and then cool off in the underground

INSIDER TIP
Dive into the deep

lake whose temperature remains a constant 18°C throughout the year. The water is so clear that the bottom of the sea feels really close, but this is a mirage – in some places it is 30m deep. There are lots of tour operators who offer day trips to this amazing underground world. *O8*

ⓨ CALES DE MALLORCA

18km from Manacor, 25 mins by car

This hotel complex was built in the 1960s and has been steadily expanding ever since. Today it can house 6,400 guests at any one time. It has an idyllic location above several small and beautiful sandy bays. However, they get so packed in high season that it is not much fun. Also, if you are staying in one of the hotels at the back, it's a fair way to the beaches. A pretty promenade and green areas make up for the lack of a town centre. *O9*

SANT LLORENÇ/ SON SERVERA

(*O-P 6-7*) **The communities of Sant Llorenç (pop. 8,300) and Son Servera (pop. 11,300), situated between Artà and Manacor in the Serra de Llevant, split the coast between Cap d'es Pinar and Punta de Sa Roca.**

The villages are connected by a very scenic road (Ma4030); most inhabitants along this coast are involved in tourism. In summer the unfinished neo-Gothic church of Son Servera houses traditional cultural events. In February, Son Servera hosts its most colourful (and prettiest) festival: the ▐ *Fira de la flor d'Ametler* (as the locals call it) or "Almond Blossom Festival". Almond products of every kind – from soaps to perfumes, creams and cakes – are brought, displayed and sold. Of course, the stars of the show are the branches covered in sweet-smelling flowers. It all takes place in *Ca s'Hereu*,

a historical stately home in the town centre – which is well worth a snoop around while you are there. More info at *visitcalamillor.com*.

SIGHTSEEING

SA PLETA FREDA
The two tireless proprietors of the gallery located directly next to the church in Son Servera have been exhibiting exciting art for the past 40 years. The tower-like construction alone makes the gallery worth a visit. *Tue–Sat 6–9pm | C/ Pleta Freda 2*

EATING & DRINKING

ES PATÍ
This "Patio" in Sant Llorenç is a little oasis for gourmets. Felix Eschrich conjures up a delicious five-course menu for only 49 euros every day, based on what he can find fresh in the market. *Mon–Sat from 7pm | C/ Soler 22 | Sant Llorenç | tel. 9 71 83 80 14 | es-pati. com | €€*

AROUND SON SERVERA

⑩ CALA BONA/CALA MILLOR
If you are after a beach and plenty of activities to keep you busy, *Cala Bona* and *Cala Millor* (pop. 6,900) will suit you to a tee. The two resorts which merge almost seamlessly into each other are linked by a ✈ 3-km-long beach and a pretty (but concrete-

heavy) promenade. The mainly three- or four-star high-rise hotels nearly all belong to large German tour operators. The huge bay is ideal for swimming and there are plenty of leisure activities on offer, which make this an ideal resort for young families.

Numerous bars and discos, such as *Britannia*, *Sanddancers* and *Bananas*, ensure that the place stays attractive for young people too. The many cafeterias, such as *Bei Petra (Thu–Tue | €)* right on the beach promenade, have adapted to the largely German clientele here. *Migjorn Gastrobar (Wed–Mon 9.30am–midnight | Passeig Marítim 19 | tel. 6 82 44 41 72 | migjorngastrobar.com | €€)* caters to a more nationally diverse crowd. With good sea views you can chow down day or night on croquettes, pork cheeks and burgers. Everything is made fresh on the premises and they have good options for veggies too.

⑪ SA COMA

6.5km from Son Servera, 10 mins by car

Separated from Cala Millor by the natural rocky outcrop of Punta de n'Amer is the spectacularly white sandy beach of Sa Coma, which is about 1km long and has a car-free promenade running from one end to the other. The area behind it is built up to the hilt with huge hotel complexes. The one-time Michelin-starred chef Tomeu Caldentey has his restaurant in the Protur Hotel Sa Coma Playa. After many years of fine-dining cookery, he now runs a simple, more affordable, bistro-style restaurant *Tomeu Caldentey Cuiner (C/ Liles | tel. 9 71 56 96 63 | tomeucaldentey.com | €€)*. His five- to ten-course menus cost between 39 and 69 euros. There are two sittings each evening: *Wed–Sat 8pm and 10pm, Sat also 1.30pm and 4.30pm*. (⊞ P7)

Cala Millor's extensive beach makes it a popular resort for young families

THE SOUTH

PERFECTLY WHITE SAND, PERFECTLY BLUE SEA

A flat, dry expanse, it may not sound great but it describes the south of Mallorca pretty accurately – oh, and hot … very hot indeed. You won't find temperatures this warm in many other parts of the island.

The towns of Llucmajor and Campos share the plain, while the municipality of Santanyí in the southeast forms part of the gentle foothills of the Serra de Llevant. This is farming country and, especially in the area around Campos, many people still earn their daily

You'll find the colours of the Caribbean at Es Trenc

bread from livestock farming. Blessed with magnificent, white sand dunes and a turquoise sea, the beautiful beaches of S'Estanyol, Sa Ràpita and Colònia de Sant Jordi could almost be in the Caribbean, and in the autumn and winter, they are ideal spots for long coastal walks. The small island of Carbrera (reached by regular ferries) is home to the "Blue Cave" – where the particular shade of deep blue never ceases to amaze visitors.

THE SOUTH

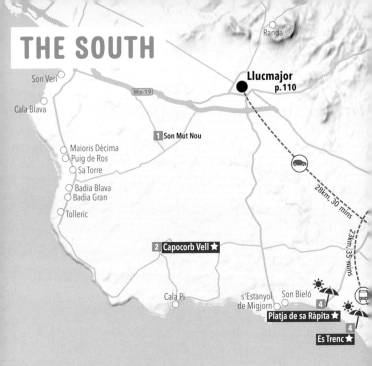

Randa

Son Verí

Cala Blava

Ma-19

Llucmajor
p. 110

1 Son Mut Nou

Maioris Dècima
Puig de Ros
Sa Torre

28km, 30 mins

Badia Blava
Badia Gran

23km, 35 mins

Tolleric

2 Capocorb Vell ★

Cala Pi

s'Estanyol
de Migjorn

Son Bieló

4
Platja de sa Ràpita ★

4
Es Trenc ★

Colònia de Sant Jordi

Cabrera ★

MARCO POLO HIGHLIGHTS

★ **CAPOCORB VELL**
Impressive remnants of life 3,500 years
ago ➤ p. 111

★ **ES TRENC/PLATJA DE SA RÀPITA**
A heavenly beach stretching as far as the
eye can see ➤ p. 113

★ **CALA FIGUERA**
A romantic fishing village unlike
anywhere else on the island ➤ p. 116

★ **PARC NATURAL MONDRAGÓ**
Emerald-green swimming coves in a
conservation area ➤ p. 117

★ **CABRERA**
The boat trip to this offshore national
park lasts about two hours ➤ p. 118

LLUCMAJOR

(▢ J9) **Llucmajor (pop. 35,500) is important to the history of the island as the place where, in 1349, the last Mallorcan king, Jaume III, was killed by the troops of his cousin Pedro IV of Aragon, sealing the fate of the independent kingdom of Mallorca.**

A monument on *Plaça Espanya* commemorates these events. A second monument nearby *(Carrer Bisbe Taxaqet)* is dedicated to the town's most important craft: shoemaking. On Wednesdays, Fridays and Sundays the vegetable market on the pretty, pedestrianised main square showcases other products that keep the inhabitants of Llucmajor going financially. If you arrive by car, park as soon as you find a space along the main road and walk the rest of the way.

The town's tourist board site *(visit llucmajor.com)* have put together some great walks and bike rides around the town and its surrounding area, which can be downloaded for free and are available in English.

EATING & DRINKING

CAFÈ ARÀBIC

Since 1994, tapas, sandwiches *(llonguets)* and simple Mallorcan dishes have been served in this café hidden away in a corner of the large town square. It has a cosy old-school feel and a large terrace. *Mon–Sat 9am–4pm | C/ Constitució 4 | tel. 9 71 12 10 01 | cafearabic.es | €€*

SHOPPING

JUST SU AQUÍ

A perfect little shop if you're looking for authentic Mallorcan souvenirs. From delicious and easily packable morsels and bottles of local wines and spirits to regional crafts, such as hand-woven baskets and cutlery with traditional tongue designs, their selection covers just about everything. *Daily 10am–1.30pm, Mon–Wed and Fri/Sat also 5–8pm | C/ del Bisbe Taixequet 81 | just-su-aqui.business.site*

MAYKA ZAPATERÍA 🐷

Shoe shopping as the locals do! Smart shoes at bargain prices. *Mon–Fri 9.30am–1.30pm and 5–8pm | C/ del Bisbe Taixequet 107*

AROUND LLUCMAJOR

◼ SON MUT NOU

9km from Llucmajor, 15 mins by car
A visit to the fig finca will spark a newfound interest in this fruit. A Mallorcan pharmacist is living out his passion here, and he has planted around 3,000 trees from more than 1,300 global fig varieties. Take a tour to find out just why these little fruits are so fascinating; in the late summer you can also sample the sweet figs as part of the tour. The finca produces 21 different products using figs, from jams to bread

INSIDER TIP
We do love a figgy beer

Mmm, very tasty! Over 800 varieties of fig can be found on the fig farm Son Mut Nou

and coffees and teas. It even has a range of fig wine and beer. A special place! *Tue, Thu, Sat 8am–1pm | admission free, group tours can be booked in advance for 8 euros/pers (incl. samples) | exit 18 on the Ma19 | Camí d'es Palmer | tel. 6 46 63 32 59 | sonmutnou.com | ⏱ 1–2 hrs | ⊞ H9*

2 CAPOCORB VELL ★

13km from Llucmajor, 20 mins by car
Arguably Mallorca's best-preserved Talaiotic settlement dates back to around 1400 BCE. Prepare to be impressed by the ruined *talaiot* several storeys high and by the large number of preserved stone foundation walls which show the extent of this former residential and defensive complex. *Fri–Wed 9am–5pm | admission 3 euros | talaiotscapocorbvell.com | ⏱ 1 hr | ⊞ H10*

CAMPOS

(⊞ K–L 9–10) **The dead straight streets of Campos are normally so deserted that the whole place seems to be asleep. However, on Thursdays and Saturdays it wakes up for its large market.**

Campos is said to have already existed in Roman times. The street leading to the municipal salt stores and the beaches along the south coast are flanked by fields where *alfalfa* (lucerne) and *tàperes* (capers) are cultivated. The huge livestock and dairy industries here make Campos a centre of the island's agricultural sector.

Someone alert Don Quixote! Windmills are still in operation near Campos

SIGHTSEEING

SANT JULIÀ

The star attraction in this parish church is the painting of *Santo Cristo de la Paciencia* by Bartolomé Murillo (1618–82). The best time to visit the church is for Mass, but it is also open on Saturdays from 10am–1pm.

EATING & DRINKING

MOLI DE VENT

Fans of mills will be captivated by this pretty, perfectly restored restaurant in a mill. It dates back to 1873 and has its own garden terrace. The couple who run the place offer fresh, seasonal cuisine in the beautiful vaults, with starters costing 8 –12 euros and mains 15–27 euros. *Thu–Tue 7-11pm | C/ Nord 34 | tel. 9 71 16 04 41 | moli-de-vent.com | €€*

SA CANOVA

Traditional seasonal cuisine with exquisite ingredients. The fish all comes from local fishermen and the fruit and vegetables are grown in their very own garden. *Daily 1.15-3.45pm, Tue–Sat also 8.15-10.45pm | Ronda Estació 18 | tel. 9 71 65 02 10 | FB: restaurantsacanova | €€*

SHOPPING

The village shows its most charming side every Saturday morning, when anyone who has something to sell – from farmers, to artisans and scrap dealers – gathers on the market square. The atmosphere is always delightfully relaxed and there are plenty of treasures to buy and take home with you.

POMAR

This bakery has been an institution on the island since 1902. The most popular items made here are the *ensaïmadas, cocas* and the homemade chocolates.

INSIDER TIP
Settle in for the long haul

Since everything they sell is so delicious, you may as well order yourselves a *café con leche* and then try as many of their tasty creations as possible. *Daily 6.30am–9pm | C/ Plaça 20–22 | (almost) opposite the church | pomaronline.com*

AROUND CAMPOS

❸ ARTESTRUZ 👀

7km from Campos, 10 mins by car
On this ostrich farm near Campos, you can get up close to these strange birds and see how they bring up their chicks.Brave kids (and adults) can feed the grown birds and if your kids have no fear whatsoever, they can

INSIDER TIP
Giddy-up ostrich!

try taking one for a ride *(max. weight 50 kg | 40 euros incl. T-shirt)* under the watchful eyes of professional handlers. You can buy many ostrich souvenirs at the shop, including huge fresh ostrich eggs for a slightly unusual family omelette back home. *Daily 10.15am–5pm | adults 12 euros, children 4–12 7 euros | exit Ctra. Llucmajor-Ses Salines, at Km40 | artestruzmallorca.com | ▱ K10*

❹ ES TRENC/PLATJA DE SA RÀPITA ★ 🌴

11km from Campos, 15 mins by car
This is the closest Mallorca gets to the Caribbean. Unspoilt by buildings, the two natural beaches *Es Trenc* and *Platja de sa Ràpita* seamlessly meld into one another. About 5km long, Es Trenc is considered one of Mallorca's most beautiful beaches (and the only one in that list which has dunes). In winter it is generally wonderfully empty (especially as the beach bars have to be taken down in the cooler months) and perfect for long walks along the seashore with the scent of the ocean and a fresh breeze accompanying you all the way.

In the summer it is a different story. It gets so crowded that the car parks *(daily 9am–9pm | day ticket 7 euros, afternoon ticket 4 euros)* are often full. Park at the yacht harbour of Sa Ràpita to be sure to get your day at the beach off to a relaxed start. You can take the free bus from there to Es Trenc, with regular departures between 10am and 6.30pm (it runs 11 times a day).

Speaking of relaxed: the young proprietors of the restaurant *S'Oratge (March–Sept Tue–Sun 12–11pm; Oct only Tue and Thu–Sat; closed Nov–Feb | C/ Llevant 56 | Sa Ràpita | tel. 9 71 64 05 89 | soratge.net | €)* offer light cuisine with grilled vegetables, fish and meat, all served in a casual atmosphere. An affordable set menu is available at lunchtime (with veggie alternatives), in the evenings the menu includes cocktails and creative plays on the classic *Pa-amb-oli.* ▱ K11

5 BALNEARIO SAN JUAN DE LA FONT SANTA

10km from Campos, 10 mins by car
Mallorca's only hot spring has been ably incorporated into the grand spa hotel *Font Santa (exit Ctra. Campos–Colònia San Jordi, at Km8.2 | tel. 9 71 65 50 16 | fontsantahotel.com)*. It offers a great range of spa treatments and a restaurant *(daily | €€€)* that uses market-fresh ingredients. Non-hotel guests pay 85 euros for a day at the spa, including lunch. Space is limited so reserve early. ▢▢ *L11*

SANTANYÍ

(▢▢ M11) **The small, lively town of Santanyí (pop. 11,600) is in an area with fabulous beaches. It therefore comes as no surprise that it is popular with tourists.**

It is a pretty place with ochre-coloured sandstone houses. And with its large number of car-free roads and many shops, bars and restaurants, it's a great place to stroll around, particularly on market days *(Wed and Sat)*.

SIGHTSEEING

SANT ANDREU

The large village church has one of the best-preserved Baroque organs in Europe (and one of the largest organs in Spain). Constructed by Jordi Bosch, one of the best-known organ builders in 18th-century Europe, it is in excellent condition. You can hear it for yourself during the 🐷 free rehearsals on Wednesdays and Saturdays at 12.30pm.

EATING & DRINKING

ANOA

Meals are cooked fresh every day using regional ingredients. Be sure to try the fish soup, made with saffron and served with aioli and home-made bread. *Tue–Sun 6–11pm, mid-Nov–mid-March closed | C/ de s'Aljub 32 | tel. 9 71 65 33 15 | anoa-santanyi.com | €€–€€€*

ES COC

Traditional Mallorcan dishes with a modern twist, served with a smile in a pretty town house and at fair prices. The daily set menu at 18.50 euros is good value. *Mon–Sat 1–3.30pm and 7–10pm | C/ Aljub 37 | tel. 9 71 64 16 31 | restaurantescoc.com | €€*

SA BOTIGA

This café with playful Mediterranean décor is right next to the church. It is a perfect pit stop at any time of the day as the owners do not take an afternoon siesta. *Daily 9am–midnight | tel. 9 71 16 30 15 | sabotiga-santanyi.com | €–€€*

SHOPPING

ECOTECA/L'ARÇ NATURA

Strong sustainable standards. A growing number of Mallorcans are trying to find ways to live more sustainably. Two organic grocery stores reflect this change. *L'Arç Natura (Mon–Sat 9.30am–1pm and Mon–Fri 4.30–7.30pm | C/*

Bernat Vidal Tomàs 23) sells fresh produce from the island, while the *Ecoteca (Mon–Sat 10am–2pm, Mon–Wed, Fri also 4.30–7.30pm | C/ Centre 6)* also sells natural cosmetics and novel gifts.

TRACES

Come here for unusual and affordable fashion and accessories created by Italian, French and Spanish labels. *Check website for opening hours | C/ Sebastià Vila 9–11 | traces-santanyi.com*

WEEKLY MARKET

Stroll through the inviting weekly market featuring numerous Mallorcan products in the around the church in the town centre *(Wed and Sat)*. The surrounding boutiques are also open on market days.

AROUND SANTANYÍ

⑥ CALA DE SA COMUNA/CALA S'AMUNIA

8km from Santanyí, 15 mins by car

A footpath (about 20 minutes) connects the two natural bays of Cala de Sa Comuna and Cala S'Amunia. Devoid of any infrastructure and not that easy to find, these represent arguably the last beach idylls on Mallorca's eastern coast that are accessible by land. Access to Cala S'Amunia is by a set of steep steps down to the sea (on a bend in the village, to the left of a private house). 𝔐 M11–12

INSIDER TIP
Paradise found!

A fisherman prepares for the next day's catch in Cala Figuera

7 CALA SANTANYÍ 🌴 👙

3.5km from Santanyí, 5–10 mins by car

White sands and shallow waters, this beach is perfect for families with children and anyone who loves snorkelling. 𝔐 M11

8 CALA FIGUERA ⭐

5km from Santanyí, 10 mins by car

This resort to the southeast of Santanyí, might not have a beach, but it is instead the most idyllic fishing port on the island. It gets particularly interesting down at the quay between around 3 and 5pm on weekdays when the fishermen return with their day's catch.

INSIDER TIP
A taste of Mallorca's past

All that looking at fish made you hungry? *Bon-Bar (Tue–Sun 10am–midnight | C/ Verge del Carme 27 | tel. 6 73 79 59 69 | €€)* sits directly above the harbour and has great views of the boat traffic below. *L'Arcada (Thu–Tue 12–10pm | C/ del Carme 80 |tel. 9 71 64 50 32 | €€)* on one of the main streets also has a sea view and serves excellent seafood among its tapas. Finally, *Pura Vida (breakfast 10am–1pm, à la carte 1–10pm | C/ Tomarinar 25 | tel. 9 71 16 55 71 | pura-vida-mallorca.com | €€–€€€)* sits 15m up on the cliffs at the southern edge of the village. It consists of a restaurant, a bistro and a bar spread over two floors with stunning sea views. *N11*

9 S'ALQUERÍA BLANCA

5km from Santanyí, 5-10 mins by car
Take a rest in this sleepy village, have a sit down in the tiny village square at *Bar Nou (Wed-Mon 1-3pm and 6.30-10.30pm | Plaça de Sant Josep 20 | tel. 9 71 53 00 05 | €-€€)* or head to the neighbouring restaurant *Sa Plaça (Wed-Mon 1-11pm | Plaça de Sant Josep 23 | tel. 9 71 16 40 22 | €€)* and while away the hours. *N10*

10 PARC NATURAL MONDRAGÓ ★

6km from Santanyí, 15 mins by car
The *Cala Mondragó* with fine sand and azure water owes its protected status to the GOB environmental organisation. The bay is not very built up but at the height of summer it can get very busy indeed!

The easiest way to get to the neighbouring Cala S'Amarador is directly from Santanyí. An *information centre (Mon-Fri 8am-3pm | free admission | tel. 9 71 18 10 22)* provides details about the natural park, which is home to rare and endangered species. You can explore the park on foot or by bike. *N11*

11 CALA D'OR/PORTOPETRO

12km from Santanyí, 15 mins by car
Built in the Ibizan style with white-washed houses framed by colourful climbing flowers, these two holiday resorts have nearly merged together. While *Cala d'Or* has very well-developed tourist infrastructure, the harbour village of *Portopetro* has preserved a bit of its laid-back character.

Cala d'Or has half a dozen small beaches. On the harbour, the fairly basic *Cafetería La Caracola (daily 7.30am-midnight | Passeig d'es Port 40 | tel. 9 71 65 70 13 | lacaracolaportopetro.com | €-€€)* serves no-frills regional cuisine. The best fresh fish and a sumptuous six-course tasting menu with harbour views for 69.50 euros can be had at *Port Petit (Wed-Mon 1-3pm and 7-11pm | C/ d'en Perico Pomar | tel. 9 71 64 30 39 | portpetit.com | €€€)*. *N11*

SES SALINES

(*L11)* **Once a sleepy village, Ses Salines (pop. 4,860 including all the surrounding farms), at the very bottom of the hot south, has recently woken up and is transforming itself into a quieter tourist village.**

Three local factors are contributing to this change: first, its glorious beaches – some of which are protected; second, the hotel resort of Colònia de Sant Jordi; and third, the salt lakes. The huge *S'Avall* estate belonging to the March banking family also forms part of the municipality.

Some good restaurants and cafés have opened up along the main village street, including *Cassai (daily 11am-midnight | C/ Sitjar 5 | tel. 9 71 62 97 21 | cassai.es | €€)*. There are a range of interesting shops too.

AROUND SES SALINES

SIGHTSEEING

BOTANICACTUS

With over 10,000 types of cacti from all over the world, and the perfect Mediterranean climate for them, this complex, covering 5,000m², claims to be Europe's largest botanical garden. What is certainly true is that since its opening in 1989 the garden with its artificial lake and restaurant has become a refreshing oasis in the hot south. *Daily April–Aug 9am–7pm, Nov–Feb 10.30am–4.30pm March and Sept/Oct 9am–6pm | admission 10.50 euros | on the road of the village towards Santanyí (Ma6100) | botanicactus.com | ⏱ 1½ hrs*

EATING & DRINKING

CA'N BONICO

This grand building in the middle of the village dates back to the 13th century and has now been converted into a posh hotel. It is one of the oldest stately homes in the whole of Mallorca, with its roots in the era when Jaume I conquered the island. Its thick walls offered the residents of the whole village of Ses Salines protection against marauding invaders. Even if you do not stay the night here, you can get a taste of this piece of Mallorcan history by eating in its restaurant. The food is excellent (especially the meat) and it has a lovely terrace for hot summer evenings. *Daily 7–10pm | Plaça San Bartolomeu 8 | tel. 9 71 64 90 22 | hotelcanbonico.com | €€–€€€*

12 COLÒNIA DE SANT JORDI

6km from Ses Salines, 10 mins by car
This hub of tourist accommodation and second homes sits just outside Ses Salines. It's not particularly pretty, but the colourful little harbour gives it a certain romantic je ne sais quoi. From here you can set off on walks to the unspoilt beaches around Es Dolç and the heavenly beaches of Es Carbó and Ses Roquetes, further to the southeast. A young Mallorcan prepares excellent food with a lot of passion at the restaurant *Sal de Cocó (Wed–Mon, hot food 12.30–3pm and 6–11pm | Moll de Pescadors | tel. 9 71 65 52 25 | restaurantsaldecoco.com | €€)* on the harbour. Her menu changes every month based on what is in season and the ingredients all come from the local market. The dishes with freshly caught fish are especially tasty. The helpings are generous; make sure you leave some room for dessert.

The port is the starting point for charming day trips by boat to ★ *Cabrera*, the protected archipelago which boasts a castle and interesting endemic flora and fauna. A trip with *Excursions a Cabrera (tel. 9 71 64 90 34 | excursionsacabrera.es)* costs from 35 euros and includes a swim in the Blue Cave (reminiscent of Capri!) and a guided tour of the castle.

No time for that? How about looking through a window into Cabrera's underwater world instead? At the

Don't be fooled: the white peaks at Es Trenc are mountains of salt

national park's visitor centre (daily 10am–2pm and 3–6pm; June–Sept 10am–7pm; closed Dec/Jan | admission 8 euros | C/ Gabriel Roca | cvcabrera.es | ⏱ 1½ hrs) on the edge of the village you can dive down into the seawater aquarium in a panorama lift to look barracudas in the eye. After that, you can head up to the lookout tower. But don't run upstairs too quickly: take a break and have a look at the maritime wall mosaic first. 📖 K11

INSIDER TIP
Look a barracuda in the eye

⓭ SALINES D'ES TRENC

7km from Ses Salines, 10 mins by car

Dazzling white mountains in the middle of the open plains of the island's south? That is not a mirage but a centuries-old saltworks whose high salt hills can be spotted from afar. In the area along the road to Es Trenc, you can enjoy a riot of colours in the summer: pink water, white salt mountains and blue sky. In the colder months, many migratory birds come here and, from August to April, flamingos stroll through the water. In the summer you can watch the salt harvest. But don't forget a hat and sunglasses.

After the guided tour, you can get coffee, ice cream or sangria at the snack bar and salty souvenirs (including oils and vinegars) at the gift shop. *Tours every day; for times check the website | 8 euros | exit Ctra. Campos–Colònia de Sant Jordi, at Km8.5 | tel. 9 71 65 53 06 | salinasdestrenc. com | 📖 K11*

THE CENTRE

EXPERIENCE THE EVERYDAY

Es Pla, "the plain", is what they call the fertile centre of the island. At the beginning of the 1970s, Mallorca's former cereal basket endured a major crisis, but the island's centre has now found a new identity with organic farming, crafts and viniculture.

Today, excellent wines are made in bodegas in Petra *(Miquel Oliver, Can Coleto)*, Algaida *(Can Majoral)* and Porreres *(Mesquida Mora, Can Feliu)*. For some resident farmers, the appearance of the words *agroturisme* and *turismo rural* in the late 1980s was like a miracle.

Wine is the focus of life in Binissalem

Since then, many have become part-time hoteliers in addition to working in the fields. The softly undulating landscape is criss-crossed by narrow paved roads connecting the villages. This is an area for discovering disused wells, pretty, wayside crosses and vicarages, as well as chapels, hermitages and monasteries. While the now-widened Ma15 from Palma to Manacor attracts a lot of traffic, it is still worth using to get to rewarding destinations such as Algaida, Montuïri and Vilafranca along the way.

THE CENTRE

Caimari
Selva
Mancor de la Vall
Orient
Biniamar
Lloseta
Inca
p. 124

Alaró **3**

23km, 30 mins

2 Binissalem

Consell

ESPAÑA

Santa Maria del Camí

Sencelles
p. 126

es Caülls

Es Figueral - Can Farineta

Biniali

Cas Canar

Sant Marçal

Pòrtol

Santa Eugènia

s'Hostalot

Pina

MARCO POLO HIGHLIGHTS

★ **SINEU MARKET**
Every Wednesday: shop at Mallorca's largest market ➤ p. 127

★ **PUIG DE RANDA**
Stunning views from Mallorca's only table mountain ➤ p. 129

★ **ELS CALDERERS**
Deep insights into life in feudal times, for young and old ➤ p. 131

★ **ERMITA DE BONANY**
Meet an eighth-century peasant Madonna and enjoy sweeping views across the heart of the island ➤ p. 133

Algaida
p. 128

es Pil·larí

Ses Cadenes
Bellavista

Son Verí

Randa

Puig de Randa ➤

Llucmajor

Cala Blava

Ma-19

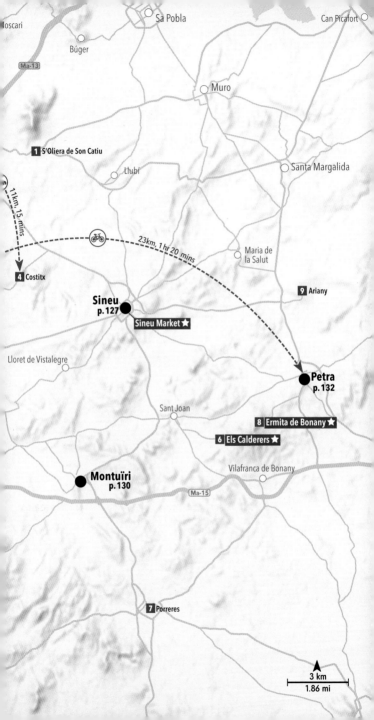

INCA

(𝄢 J5) **Inca, Mallorca's fourth-largest town (pop. 30,600), is much more interesting than its reputation would have you think.**

Although it suffers from urban sprawl at the edges, the recently spruced-up centre makes up for it with leafy squares, quiet streets and lots of good bars and restaurants, in particular between the Plaça Santa Major, which is fringed by cafés, and the town hall square. The town, a centre of shoemaking since the Catalan conquest, is still well known for producing leather goods, even if the factory

Learn how shoes are made in Inca

shops are all located outside the town centre.

Excellent bakeries beckon in the pleasantly car-free centre. Another good choice are the *cellers*, cellar pubs serving down-to-earth, hearty local cuisine. The weekly market on a Thursday might be the island's largest, but it is also very touristy. One big draw here each year is the annual *dijous bou*, the big harvest festival market on the second Thursday in November. The town is full to bursting for the whole week and finding a parking space will be nigh on impossible if you come by car.

EATING & DRINKING

CELLERS

The most famous and most expensive one is the pretty *Can Amer (daily 1–4pm, Mon–Sat also 7–11pm | C/ Pau 39 | tel. 9 71 50 12 61 | celler-canamer. es | €€)*. *Sa Travessa (Sat–Thu 1–4pm and 7–11pm | C/ de sa Murtra 16 | tel. 9 71 50 00 49 | €€)* is very authentic and has its own patio. *Can Ripoll (Tue–Sun 12.30–3.30pm, Tue–Sat also 7.30–11pm | C/ Armengol 4 | tel. 9 71 50 00 24 | restaurantcanripoll.com | €€)* is the real deal (with fair prices to match). *Can Marrón (Mon–Sat 12.30–3.30pm and 8–11pm | C/ RectorRayo 7 | tel. 971504160 | €€)* offers traditional cuisine among old wine barrels.

SA FÁBRICA

This old leather factory has been converted into a trendy cultural centre with an extremely modern restaurant. It is run by two very talented young chefs (one German, one Spanish). Their three-course lunch menu costs just 16.50 euros. *Tue–Sat 1–3.30pm and 7.30–10.30pm | Gran Vía de Colón 28 | tel. 9 71 41 25 07 | safabrica.es | €–€€*

SHOPPING

Asinca, Camper, Farrutx, Lotusse and *Munper* are the leather goods factories that sell their wares along the Carretera Palma–Inca. It is a good place to pick up handmade fashionable and smart shoes (or leather jackets) for a very fair price. For an extensive shopping tour head for the traffic-calmed centre around the market square at Carrer Pau where there are more than 200 shops.

AROUND INCA

◻ S'OLIERA DE SON CATIU

5.5km from Inca, 10 mins by car
This very modern *tafona* (oil mill) has a large restaurant which serves excellent *pa amb olis (8–14 euros)*, made with their own oil (obviously) and combined with a range of unusual ingredients, including squid. They sell a full range of Mallorcan oil products.

If you want to sample some of their oils, the mill has its own restaurant. Offering breakfast and lunch every day, and dinner at the weekend,

they incorporate their delicious oil into every dish they can. Oil tastings are also available. *Ctra. Llubí-Inca at the roundabout (Ctra. Muro) | tel. 9 71 87 46 02 | soncatiu.com | ◰ K6*

◻ BINISSALEM

6km from Inca, 10 mins by car
The area around this prettily restored small town (pop. 8,100) was the first region on Mallorca whose wines were granted "Denominació de Origen" (DO) status for their certified origin. The largest local bodega is the *Bodega José L Ferrer (tel. 9 71 51 10 50 | vinos ferrer.com)* on the road to Palma. By phone, you can book guided tours *(17 euros/pers)* of the cellar and the vineyards. The price includes a tasting where you will be served Menorcan cheese and Mallorcan biscuits – with jam made from their own grapes – along with your wines. *◰ H5*

◻ ALARÓ

11km from Inca, 15 mins by car
Alaró (pop. 5,300) is a welcoming village with Arabic origins set among pretty gardens and almond tree groves. In 1901, it became the very first place on Mallorca to get electricity.

At the centre, the market square with church, town hall and bars also boasts the ⚑ *Ca na Juanita* bakery founded in 1910 and famous for its *ensaïmadas*. On Saturdays (market day), the traders loudly sell their wares all around the square. However, they are often drowned out by

Leave the bustle behind and enjoy the solitude of Castell d'Alaró

the organ (built 1758) in ❧ *Santo Batomeu*, where a free concert takes place every Saturday at 12.30pm. Fans of contemporary art should pay a visit to the *Galerie Addaya (C/ Alexandre Rosselló 10 | addaya-art. com)*. The village's cultural centre. *Casal Son Tugores (ajalaro.net)* also runs very good free exhibitions.

The mountain restaurant *Es Verger (Tue–Sun 10am–8pm | Camino del Castillo de Alaró s/n | tel. 9 71 18 21 26 | €)*, above Alaró, is famous for its lamb shoulder and snails served by a cosy fireplace. A glass of simple local wine is the perfect accompaniment. If you are going to take on the hairpin-heavy drive up there, make sure to reserve in advance. From the restaurant you can hike to the *Castell d'Alaró* in about an hour where you can also get something to eat *(daily | tel. 9 71 94 05 03 |€)*. Their menu is very basic

– everything has to be transported up by donkey – but they nearly always have delicious *pa amb oli* and some local pastries. ▦ *G–H5*

SENCELLES

(▦ J6) **The charm of this region to the west of the Pla lies in the many hamlets surrounding Sencelles (pop. 3,150), all of which have been sensitively restored.**

In Sencelles itself the traditions of making bagpipes and of cultivating figs have been preserved to this day. It is a very pretty place with a lovely, relaxed approach to life – Mallorcan style – and a very impressive church. Every Saturday a mini market appears around the church. It could not get much more idyllic.

EATING & DRINKING

SA CUINA DE N'AINA

A Mallorcan family business in which mother Aina cooks alongside her daughter-in-law Laura, while son David is the sommelier and runs the front of house. Good suckling pig. *Daily 7.30–10.30pm, Wed–Sun also 12.30–3.30pm; Oct–May Mon evening and Tue closed | C/ Rafal 31 | tel. 9 71 87 29 92 | sacuinadenaina.com | €€*

AROUND SENCELLES

4 COSTITX

5km from Sencelles, 10 mins by car
This pretty village (pop. 1,250), which sits in a commanding position on a hill, was made famous by the find, in 1894, of three bronze bull heads dating back to Talaiotic times. The site where they were discovered, *Son Corró (always open | just before you get to the village on the road from Sencelles)*, is open to the public. The *Caps de Bou*, whose design is so minimalist they could be contemporary, are today on display in the Museo Arqueológico Nacional in Madrid.

Not far from Son Corró you will also find the Balearics' only observatory, the *Observatori Astronòmic de Mallorca (admission 10 euros | Camí de Son Bernat, well signposted | tel. 6 49 99 77 52 or 6 95 07 33 12 | oam reservas@gmail.com)*. Generally open on Fridays and Saturdays from 8pm in

summer and 7pm in winter *(opening times frequently change so ring ahead to check)*, it also holds frequent events, for example, during the nights in August when most falling stars are visible. A perfect way to round off a day of hard holidaying. ⬜ K6

SINEU

(⬜ K–L6) **Of all the villages in the centre, Sineu (pop. 3,300) is the most famous. This is mainly due to the ★ market every Wednesday, which has been held since 1306 and is the largest of its kind on Mallorca.**

Get there very early in the morning before the tourist buses arrive. What makes this market so special is that you can see animal breeds that are only found on Mallorca, from black pigs and red sheep to particular types of hen and magnificent cockerels. There are also many dog breeds you won't find elsewhere, from the very lively Rateros to the Ca de Bestiar, a big dark sheepdog. But there is much more to Sineu than just its market. Its origins are in the Talaiotic-Roman era; later, it was one of the island's six main Moorish settlements; then, in medieval times, it was chosen by King Jaume II to be his primary residence.

SIGHTSEEING

MARE DE DEU DELS ANGELS

A broad flight of steps leads up to the massive church, whose exterior masks a surprisingly delicate interior. A winged bronze lion guards the church and its 16th-century statue of the Virgin. The *Casa Rectoral* (rectory) *(Wed at market times from roughly 8am-1.30pm)* exhibits nearly 800 ceramic objects dating back to the 12th and 13th centuries.

EATING & DRINKING

CELLER ES GROP
A small simple but very traditional *celler* with friendly service. *Tue–Sun 9.30am-4pm and 7pm-midnight | C/ Major 18 | in the pedestrianised central area | tel. 9 71 52 01 87 | €*

CELLER SON TOREO
Son Toreo, a simple and very authentic *celler*, has a very loyal pack of regulars. *Tue–Sun 9am-4pm and 7.30-11pm | C/ Son Torelló 1 | tel. 9 71 52 01 38 | €*

DAICA
Excellent restaurant in the small hotel by the church in the neighbouring village of Llubí (7km away). David Ribas and Caterina Pieras create delicious food using the very freshest produce. They also have a charming courtyard. *Wed–Mon 7.30-110pm | C/ de la Farinera 7 | mobile tel. 6 86 00 16 04 | daica.es | €*

ALGAIDA

(⮂ J7) **The first thing both locals and tourists notice in the Pla's largest town after Inca (it could easily be a large-ish village; pop. 5,430) is the number of restaurants along the Ma15: it is not for nothing that Algaida is known as "foodie town".**

The restaurants on this road are carrying on a long tradition that dates back to when stagecoaches once stopped here. The food in most of them is every bit as traditional although the town itself is rather unspectacular.

SIGHTSEEING

VIDRIOS DE ARTE GORDIOLA ⛱
The island's oldest glass-blowing establishment has been going since 1719. You can watch the glass blowers at work and visit the glass museum next door. *Factory opening hours Mon–Fri 9.30am-1.30pm and 3-6.30pm, Sat 9am-noon; Museum/Shop Mon–Sat 9am-6.30pm, Sun 9.30am-1.30pm | free admission | on the Ma15, at the western edge of town (Km19) | gordiola.com*

EATING & DRINKING

CAL DIMONI
Huge, rustic and very Mallorcan: this is a veteran amongst Algaida's eateries. On a Sunday, though, it can get horrendously busy! *Thu–Tue noon-midnight | Ma15, exit at Km21 | tel. 9 71 66 50 35 | restaurantecaldimoni. com | €€*

HOSTAL D'ALGAIDA ⚑
Cosy restaurant-cum-shop selling its own products and serving them in regional dishes, good atmosphere. A

place to try *pa amb oli* – with ham, cheese, pickled samphire, capers and olives. *Daily 8am–midnight | Ma15, exit at Km21 | tel. 9 71 66 51 09 | €–€€*

hermitage with sweeping views across the plain from Llucmajor to the archipelago of Cabrera has been restored, the sandstone rock stabilised, and

It's hot work creating Gordiola's glassware

AROUND ALGAIDA

🟥 PUIG DE RANDA ★

5km from Algaida, 10 mins by car

At 542m, Mallorca's only table mountain is the highest elevation on the Pla. It is worth strolling through the cobbled alleyways in the village of *Randa* (pop. 110), which sits at the foot of the mountain. Above Randa, the mountain road leads first of all to the *Santuari de Nostra Senyora de Gràcia*, the lowest of three monasteries. This abandoned 15th-century

parking spaces made available. About 1km further up the mountain, you will come to the *Santuari de Sant Honorat*, which was founded at the end of the 14th century and is inhabited by monks to this day. The only part that is accessible to visitors is the 17th-century chapel. At first glimpse, the anticipated "wow" factor of the view from the top is lessened somewhat by radar masts on the summit, but the sweeping views from the terrace of the *Santuari de Nostra Senyora de Cura* more than make up for it. In terms of cultural history, this is the most important of the three monasteries. In 1263, the Santuari was the chosen retreat of *Ramón Llull (see page 19)* after he gave up his hedonistic life at the Mallorcan court. Today, a classroom in the old school in Cura on the mountain houses a *Ramón Llull Museum (daily 10am–1.30pm and 3–6pm; Nov–mid-Feb until 5pm | admission 5 euros)*. In

the cafeteria, make sure you try the Licor Randa, a herbal liqueur which you can only get up here. If you want somewhere to stay but don't need lots of luxury, 33 of the old monastic cells have been converted into simple rooms. Guests also receive meals from the monastery's kitchen *(tel. 9 71 12 02 60 | €)*. ⊞ J8

MONTUÏRI

(⊞ K7) **With its sturdy parish church and 19 mill towers, which attest to its long agricultural tradition, this village (pop. 2,830) of Arabic origin sprawls over a hilltop and is pretty as a picture.**

Today the village owes its fame to breeding partridges and to the fact that, in 1995, the famous *Perlas Orquídeas* pearl company transferred one of its factories here. A stroll around the *plaça* (with the weekly market on a Monday) leads past well-maintained houses, wells, wayside crosses and mills, as well as the broad flight of steps in front of the parish church of *Sant Bartomeu*, which dates back to the 16th to 18th centuries. There are very good brochures with information for your walk available in a variety of languages in the town hall.

If you want to learn a bit more about village life here, the local council has set up village tours which start at the *Son Fornés* Talaiotic site and take in the local history museum before heading into the village itself. As part of the tour, you will see an old school *celler*, a traditional village house as well as a mill. You will learn a lot about traditional processes for the milling of wheat. *Groups from 10 euros/pers.; smaller groups on request (min. 4 participants) 12 euros/pers | book early by calling 9 71 64 41 69*

EATING & DRINKING

SON BASCOS

This local institution is revered for its quail (*cordoniz* in Spanish or *guàtleres* in Catalan) specialities. It also has a pleasant garden to sit in during the summer months. *Wed–Mon 8–11.30pm, Sun also 1–3.30pm | Camí Son Rubí | tel. 9 71 64 61 70 | son-bascos.business.site | €*

HORTELLA D'EN COTANET

Spacious, family-run country inn located between Montuïri, Sant Joan and Vilafranca serving local dishes. While you wait for your dinner on the terrace, you gaze out over a landscape of fields and forests. In the summer, jazz concerts are performed on the meadow. *June–Oct Tue–Sun 1–11pm, otherwise check website for opening times | exit 34 on Ctra. Palma–Manacor*

There are 19 traditional mills in the hilltop village of Montuïri

| 8km from Montuïri, 10 mins by car | tel. 9 71 83 21 43 | hortelladencotanet. com | €

AROUND MONTUÏRI

🿂 ELS CALDERERS ★

7km from Montuïri, 10 mins by car
This fortress-like manor house, with its own chapel, wine cellar, stables, servants' quarters and aristocratic salons, gives you an idea of feudal life, particularly if you stroll around walls which are more than 300 years old or listen to the woman in period finery playing the piano. They also have Mallorcan black pigs and in winter you can see birds of prey performing

during their falconry displays. *April–Oct 10am–6pm, Nov–March 10am–5pm | admission 9 euros | exit the Ma15 at Km37 (signposted) near Sant Joan east of Montuïri | elscalderers.com | ⏱ 2 hrs | ⊞ L7*

🿃 PORRERES

8km from Montuïri, 10 mins by car
A widening of the roads around it has made this small town (pop. 5,250) more accessible. The weekly market on a Tuesday is well worth a visit. Don't miss the impressive gallery containing contemporary art in the old hospital building, the *Museu i Fons Artístic (Tue, Sun 11am–1pm, Fri/Sat 11am–1pm and 6–8pm, summer 7–9pm | admission free | C/ d'Agustí Font | ⏱ 1–1½ hrs)*. Among the 300 pieces are two works by Salvador Dalí. The rose window and bell tower of the

parish church on the market square are impressive too. Right next to the church is *Centre (Tue–Sun 1–3.30pm and 7–11pm | tel. 9 71 64 75 47 | €)* a former theatre, which today operates as a rustic restaurant.

These days, Porreres has returned to making a living from its wine. Right in the heart of the town, you can visit the bodega *Mesquida Mora (Camí Pas des Frare | tel. 6 87 97 14 57 | mesquida mora.com)* This vineyard does not use chemical pesticides or fertilisers. In the summer ask about the concerts their owner, Bàrbara Mesquida, organises in the vineyards. If you want to learn a bit about traditional agricultural daily life on Mallorca while also sampling some delicious organic wine, pay a visit to *Can Feliu (March–Nov | Km1.2 on Camí de Sa Serra | bodegacanfeliu.com)* on a Friday. They offer a tour of their bodega with a barbecue and wine tasting

INSIDER TIP
A taste of Mallorca in a glass

afterwards *(34 euros)*. Carlos, the winemaker, also allows people to bring their own grapes to be made into wine using his equipment. *□□ L8*

PETRA

(□□ M6-7) **The narrow streets of this sleepy village (pop. 2,800) were laid out in their chequerboard pattern under Jaume I.**

Petra was called "The Luminous One" by its Arabic founders in an allusion to its Jordanian namesake. The village's second great claim to fame is its most celebrated son, Fra Juníper Serra, a Franciscan monk and missionary, who was canonised in 2015 by Pope Francis. Serra founded 21 Christian mission stations in California, some of which developed into huge cities such as San Francisco and Los Angeles.

The Ermita de Bonany is a reminder that even sunshine islands need rain

SIGHTSEEING

CASA NATAL I MUSEU JUNÍPER SERRA 🏠

Find out about the life of the missionary and saint (1713–84) in the house of his birth and the museum. *Mon, Wed, Fri 10.30am–1.30pm or by appointment | free admission, donations welcome | on the corner between C/ Barracar Alt 6 and C/ Fra Juníper Serra | tel. 6 64 36 67 22 | fundacion casaserra.org | ⏲ 1 hr*

BODEGA MIQUEL OLIVER

This bodega is over a century old and is one of the most famous on the island. Today, daughter Pilar Oliver rules the roost, having been away to study winemaking. Her dry Muscat has been crowned the best white wine in Spain. *Signposted at Km1.8 on Ctra. Petra–Santa Margalida, | miqueloliver.com*

EATING & DRINKING

CAN SALOM

A family-run restaurant which has been spoiling its guests with regional dishes since 1969. Joan Riera Salom is the owner, and it is always worth asking him about any dishes which are not on the menu. Make sure you try the house wine too. *Daily 6–11pm, Sat/Sun also 12.30–3pm | Plaça Fray Junípero Serra 4 | tel. 9 71 56 10 46 | cansalom.com | €€*

ES CELLER

There's no place quite as cosily old-fashioned and with such unique ambiance as this cellar tavern in the heart of the town. The quality of the dishes, however, oscillates between excellent and mediocre. *Daily noon–11pm | C/ de l'Hospital 46 | signposted | tel. 9 71 56 10 56 | restaurantesceller.com | €*

AROUND PETRA

🟦 ERMITA DE BONANY ★

4km from Petra, 10 mins by car

A trip to this monastery is worth making for the chubby-faced eighth-century Madonna statue and the panoramic view alone. The monastery owes its name (Good Year) to the end of a period of severe drought. At the entrance, tiled images are a reminder of the long-awaited rain and the rich harvest that followed. There is also a great picnic area under shade of tall trees. 🔲 L7

🟦 ARIANY

5km from Petra, 10 mins by car

This small village (pop. 850) just north of Petra only achieved independence from its neighbour in 1982. The village's heart is its church, whose beautiful front garden, full of blooms and boasting sweeping views, is well worth a stop. The restaurant *Ses Torres (daily 7am–midnight | tel. 9 71 83 04 29 | grcm.es/ses-torres | €)*, at the big roundabout in Ariany, serves good tapas and a good-value set meal and is a popular pit stop for truck drivers and day-trippers. 🔲 M6

DISCOVERY TOURS

Want to get under the skin of the region? Then our discovery tours provide the perfect guide – they include advice on which sights to visit, tips on where to stop for that perfect holiday snap, a choice of the best places to eat and drink and suggestions for fun activities.

❶ MALLORCA AT A GLANCE

> ➤ Discover mini "dragons" on the island of Sa Dragonera
> ➤ Wind your way up to Mallorca's highest mountains
> ➤ Party like it's going out of fashion

📍 Palma	🏁 Palma	
🔄 400km	🚗 6 days (total driving time: 7½ hrs)	

ℹ️ Information: You can only visit the island of Sa Dragonera from April to October.

Schedule a stop in Pollença as part of your tour of the island

LEAVING PALMA

Regardless of whether you're arriving by boat or plane, almost everyone's first stop is the lively capital city of ❶ Palma ➤ p. 42. On arrival, though, pick up your rental car first and save the capital itself for after you have explored the rest of the island. *Take the Ma1* to ❷ Port d'Andratx ➤ p. 63. Stroll for a while along the harbour and have a look at the yachts and fishing boats before stopping for a bite to eat at one of the many restaurants.

A WORLD OF LIZARDS & BIRDS

Drive on to the peaceful seaside resort of ❸ Sant Elm ➤ p. 64. Boats departing from here *(13 euros)* will ferry you across to the unspoilt island of ❹ Sa Dragonera ➤ p. 64 with its many birds and lizards. The crossing only takes about 20 minutes, but you should plan at least three hours for this little excursion. Once you are back on the mainland, follow the *curvy Ma10* to the sleepy hillside village of ❺ Estellencs ➤ p. 64. The village clings to the steep coastal cliffs and the sea views are all around. You can spend the night at Petit Hotel Sa Plana *(saplana.com)*.

DAY 1

❶ **Palma**
31km 30 mins

❷ **Port d'Andratx**
9km 10 mins

❸ **Sant Elm**
2km 20 mins

❹ **Sa Dragonera**
25km 45 mins

❺ **Estellencs**
24km 30 mins

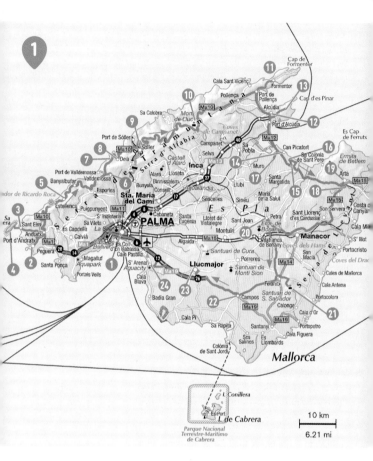

DAY 2	
❻ Valldemossa	
8km 15 mins	
❼ Son Marroig	
4km 5 mins	
❽ Deià	
11km 15 mins	

The next day, head off to ❻ Valldemossa ➤ p. 65. A visit to the charterhouse (admission 9.50 euros) is well worthwhile. Afterwards, treat yourself to a sweet and delicious *coca de patata*, which you can buy at just about every bakery, and meander through the lower part of the village.

The next part of the drive is quite spectacular with the sea to the left and olive groves and steep rocky cliffs to the right. Stop at the ❼ Son Marroig ➤ p. 68 and tour the idyllic gardens before driving past the picture-perfect houses nestled into the hills in ❽ Deià ➤ p. 67.

Continue to **⑨ Sóller** ➤ p. 69, where you can relax and enjoy an ice-cream on the patio of the Fàbrica de Gelats. Treat yourselves to a room for the night in the very swish Hotel Espléndido *(esplendidohotel.com)*.

THE BLACK MADONNA AWAITS

After breakfast, follow the *Ma10* up to the highest mountains on the island. As you wind your way up the road, the views are amazing. You will pass two reservoirs before reaching **⑩ Lluc Monastery** ➤ p. 93, which is home to the famous "Black Madonna". Drive down through forests of holm oaks to the rural town of Pollença. Your next destination is the **⑪ Formentor Peninsula** ➤ p. 92. Stop at the mirador and enjoy the fantastic view before taking a coffee break in the garden of the hotel Barceló Formentor. From here, drive on to the town of **⑫ Alcúdia** ➤ p. 85. and its medieval walls. Check into a room at the Ca'n Pere Hotel *(hotelcanpere. com)* and then stroll through the beautifully restored houses in the centre of town.

SUBMERGE YOURSELF IN THE ISLAND'S HISTORY … AND THE SEA

On the next day, it is worth making a detour up to the **⑬ Ermita de la Victoria** ➤ p. 89. You can go for a swim right below the hermitage on the small pebbly beach of S'Illot. Continue on the *Ma12* to **⑭ Can Picafort** ➤ p. 82. Check into your hotel of choice and then treat yourself to a nice lunch. In the afternoon, rent a bike at Mallorca on Bike *(daily 9am–12pm, 4.30–6pm and by appointment | rental: 10 euros/day | Ctra. Artá–Port d'Alcùdia 65b | tel. 6 32 48 77 21 | mallorcaonbike.com)*. Hop on and *cycle along the Ma12* until you come to a former country estate that now houses a **⑮ museum of island history**. Next, *follow a country path to* **⑯ Son Real** ➤ p. 83, the large Talaiotic "city of the dead". This necropolis sits directly by the sea, so you can have a second dip here. Return to Can Picafort and give back your bike. In the evening, the drive out to the gourmet restaurant **⑰ Es Casal** *(daily 7.30–10.30pm | at Km1.8 on Ctra. Santa Margalida–Alcúdia | tel. 9 71 85 27 32 | casal-santaeulalia.com | €€€)* is definitely worthwhile.

⑨ Sóller	
40km 50 mins	
DAY 3	
⑩ Lluc Monastery	
30km 35 mins	
⑪ Formentor Peninsula	
24km 30 mins	
⑫ Alcúdia	
7km 15 mins	
DAY 4	
⑬ Ermita de la Victoria	
17 km 25 mins	
⑭ Can Picafort	
5km 20 mins	
⑮ Museum of island history	
2.4km 10 mins	
⑯ Son Real	
9.5km 50 mins	
⑰ Es Casal	
26km 25 mins	

Continue exploring Talaiotic culture the following day with a visit to ⑱ Ses Païsses, an impressive settlement dating back to this period. In the lovely country town of ⑰ Artà ➤ p. 80 , *start at the parish church and follow the Way of the Cross (lined by cypresses) up to the* fortress to enjoy the amazing panoramic view.

MALLORCA'S CALIFORNIAN CONNECTION

After a break for lunch, *drive along the Ma15 into the interior of the island. Pass through Manacor and then turn onto the Ma3320*, which will bring you to the Es Pla plateau and the little town of ⑳ Petra ➤ p. 132. Explore its famous tiled lane and museum dedicated to Friar Juníper Serra, the founder of many Californian cities. Take the *Ma3310, the Ma5110 and the Ma5111* through wheat fields and vineyards to Felanitx and then continue on the *Ma4010*. Turn onto the narrow *road with lots of hairpin bends* that leads up to the holy mountain of ㉑ Sant Salvador ➤ p. 99and spend a night at the wonderful Petit Hotel Hostatgeria Sant Salvador *(santsalvadorhotel.com)*.

SNACK WITH THE LOCALS

Depart Sant Salvador the next morning and drive back to *Felanitx to get to the PM512*, which will take you to the farming village of ㉒ Campos ➤ p. 111. If you want to spend time with the locals, pop into the bakery Forn Ca'n Nadal *(C/ Estrelles 22)* for some crisp bread fresh from the wood-fired oven and tasty *ensaïmadas* (a kind of lardy cake). Or you can stop and visit the friendly artist Miquela Vidal *(C/ Pare Alzina 7 | Tel. 971652010)*. She opens her home/studio on Saturdays during the market (around

INSIDER TIP
An artist's impression

10.30am–1.30pm). Her work is lovely as is her renovated traditional village cottage. Afterwards, walk past the stalls of the weekly market in Campos. The village has carved a name for itself as a little haven for bargain-seekers with plenty of bric-a-brac, bits and bobs, and unusual souvenirs.

An abandoned monastery sits atop Sant Salvador mountain at a height of 509m

Drive on to ㉓ Llucmajor ➤ p.110. This reasonably sized town is not particularly beautiful, but it still has lots to offer visitors. *Park your car as soon as you find a space on the main road coming in* and ask for directions to the busy village square (Plaça Espanya) nearby. The square is lined with cafés and small restaurants that are perfect for relaxed people-watching. Some of the little shops are rather quaint, others are quite stylish. You can pick up walking guides to the town at the tourist information office (C/ de la Constitució 1). The guided route takes you through the middle of town from the King Jaume III memorial to the monastery.

THEN THERE'S BALLERMANN ...

It is only a stone's throw from Llucmajor to ㉔ Platja de Palma ➤ p.62 *on the Ma19*. The beach begins in Arenal, but the bay stretches over 10km to the outskirts of Palma. If you want to take a quick glance (and we don't recommend spending much more time there) at the infamous Ballermann beach section 6 which is so popular among partying German tourists, *park in*

㉓ Llucmajor
18km 45 mins

㉔ Platja de Palma
20km 1 hr 20 mins

Arenal and walk for about half an hour *along the beach promenade towards Palma.* The street named Pare Bartomeu Salvàis the middle of the legendary party area. If you want to stop for a bite to eat on the way back to the car, be wary of the tourist traps. A recommended restaurant is Casa do Pulpo *(May-Oct Wed-Mon 11am–11.15pm; Dec-April Wed-Mon 11am–4pm and 7–11.15pm; Nov closed | C/ Terral 44 | tel. 9 71 44 15 77 | €-€€).*

Your trip has now brought you back to where you started in ❶ Palma. Make sure you spend a few days exploring the capital – you won't be disappointed.

❶ Palma

❷ IN THE FOOTSTEPS OF SMUGGLERS

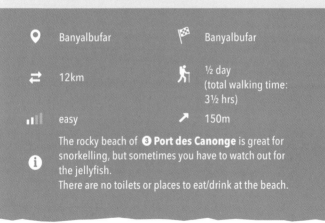

➤ Visit stunning vineyards with vines that date back to the Moorish era
➤ Hear the cliffs rumble as you walk
➤ See the island's most spectacular sunset

📍	Banyalbufar	🏁	Banyalbufar
⇄	12km	🚶	½ day (total walking time: 3½ hrs)
📶	easy	↗	150m

ℹ️ The rocky beach of ❸ **Port des Canonge** is great for snorkelling, but sometimes you have to watch out for the jellyfish.
There are no toilets or places to eat/drink at the beach.

❶ Banyalbufar
4.5km 50 mins

LET YOUR IMAGINATION RUN WILD
Leave the mountain village of ❶ Banyalbufar ➤ p. 64 and *drive eastwards. On the Ma 10, in a chicane between Km85 and 86,* you will find a car park. It is the starting point for the day's hike. The trail is marked the

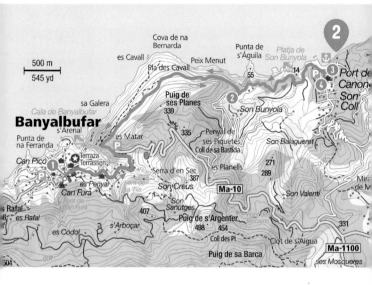

entire way with arrows on wooden stakes. Thanks to the shady forest of Aleppo pines, the hike is not too strenuous even on hot summer days. This path was used by smugglers during the Franco era to transport sacks of cigarettes, alcohol and coffee from the sea to their hideaways. Allow your imagination to take over as you follow in their footsteps.

NO-ONE DOES THIS ANYMORE

After just a few strides, you will be able to look back at Banyalbufar with its terraced fields of vegetables and Malvasia grapes dating back to Moorish times. The *trail leads through a forest of holm oaks* in which a virtually extinct trade has been kept alive in the form of a *sitga*, a circular charcoal pile with a reed-covered hut for the charcoal burners who had to be on site day and night. Also keep a lookout for the ruins of a *forn de calç*, a lime kiln, in which limestone was fired to produce lime for whitewashing houses.

Barely perceptibly, the path begins to *slope gently downhill. Continue walking for about a half an hour* until you come to a huge craggy rock face. Admire the stalactites and stalagmites in the limestone and listen to the rumbling sea. On days when the sea is restless, the wall amplifies the thunderous sound of the waves.

A BEAUTIFUL DESCENT

As you walk further along, you will eventually come to a point where bizarre, wildly romantic rock crags jut out over the sea far below with wind-bent pines clinging to them. White sea spray crashes onto the rocky beach, and every now and then a boat crosses the broad blue horizon of the sea. Far off into the distance, try to make out the shape of the small Sa Foradada peninsula. It was here that Archduke Ludwig Salvator hit land and "discovered" Mallorca. The trail continues *downhill*, past the large, 400-year-old estate of ❷ Son Bunyola. A British billionaire purchased the property in order to build a luxurious finca hotel on the site, but he never got planning permission. After Son Bunyola, you will finally find yourself at the crystal-clear sea. The pebbly beach is a paradise for snorkelling. Don't hesitate, just jump right in – by this point even those who have forgotten their trunks will want a refreshing dip!

❷ **Son Bunyola**
1.7km 30 mins

Pause to enjoy the view en route to Port des Canonge

TO THE END OF THE WORLD

You still have a bit to go. *Walk past myrtle bushes* until you reach the tiny harbour town of ❸ Port des Canonge. In the height of summer, it is a lively place, especially at the weekend when Mallorcan day trippers arrive. At other times of the year, it is virtually abandoned – which makes it all the more charming. Red rocks tower over the harbour ringed by softly rounded red stones and algae. The scent of fish and salt fill the air. Sometimes the fishermen nap in the shade of their tarpaulins. All in all, it is a peaceful place with a distinct end-of-the-world feel.

> ❸ Port des Canonge
> 70m 2 mins

By now you will have worked up an appetite and probably be in need of a rest. *Walk up the main street*, past the restaurant Toni, and grab a table at ❹ Can Madó *(Wed–Mon 10am–6pm | C/ Port des Canonge | tel. 9 71 61 05 52 | €€)*. The place is not particularly pretty but has no airs above its station either. Order a few tapas and a glass of the excellent white house wine, watch the cats milling about and allow yourself a few moments to forget that you have to *hike uphill all the way back to the car*. Nonetheless, you can rest assured knowing that you will discover entirely new vistas and plenty of other things along the trail that you missed on the way down.

> ❹ Can Madó
> 6.1km 2 hrs

ORDER A CORTADO WITH A SEA VIEW

Don't forget to wander around ❶ Banyalbufar ➤ p. 49 on your return. Nestled on the hillside, the town is busy in summer. The natural beauty of the west coast with its spectacular sunsets has meant many Mallorcans own holiday flats here. Good coffee and cake (to be enjoyed with a sea view) are on offer on the main road at Café Bellavista *(daily 10am–10pm | C/ del Comte de Sallent 15 | tel. 9 71 61 80 04 | restaurant-i-cafe-bellavista. business.site | €€)*. Malvasia wine from the village is sold next door.

> ❶ Banyalbufar

❸ THE COUNTRY & ITS PEOPLE: FARMERS, VINTNERS & FISHERMEN

➤ Visit a bustling market with pigs, hens and sheep
➤ Take in two lighthouses on foot
➤ Leap into the waves at two wild beaches

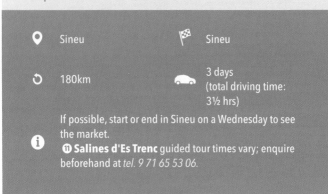

📍 Sineu   🏁 Sineu

🕐 180km   🚗 3 days
                              (total driving time:
                              3½ hrs)

ℹ️ If possible, start or end in Sineu on a Wednesday to see the market.
⓫ Salines d'Es Trenc guided tour times vary; enquire beforehand at *tel. 9 71 65 53 06.*

DAY 1
❶ Sineu
10km 15 mins

ISLAND CENTRAL

The starting point for this tour is ❶ Sineu ➤ p. 127, at the geographical heart of the island. Farmers from far and wide flock to the island's oldest and most important market held here on Wednesdays. If you get there really early, you can witness traders and farmers haggling over all manner of livestock.

FOLLOW THE WINE

Around 10am, when entire coachloads of tourists pour into the market, you should already be on your way to Sant Joan, *7km to the south. In the centre of the village, follow the sign to Els Calderers*. It leads to the impressive estate of ❷ Els Calderers ➤ p. 131, which has been converted into a finca museum. A huge wine cellar attests to the former glory of the winemaking trade that flourished here until a blight of phylloxera hit at the turn of the 20th century. Recently, efforts have been made to revive the vineyards. An enormous granary on the upper floor marks the switchover from wine to wheat that took place after the grapes failed. It also

❷ Els Calderers
17km 20 mins

displays the estate's other agricultural products. Make sure you take advantage of the wine tastings on offer.

As you drive *further south*, you will pass through the municipality of Vilafranca. Smoke-blackened kilns and piles of *tejas* (tiles) bear witness to the ancient (and still practised) trade of brick-making. Until now, fields of wheat and plantations of trees bearing almonds, figs and carob have lined the road. But once you *cross the Ma15*, vineyards take over. The area around Petra, Porreres and Felanitx is one of the main cultivation areas for white wine grapes.

Cala Figuera

BROWSE FOR CERAMICS AT NIGHT

You will soon come to the country town of ❸ Felanitx ➤ p. 98 , with its characteristic stumpy mill sitting above the centre. It is now, finally, time for lunch. The main street, Carrer Major, is at the heart of the town. For upscale cuisine at reasonable prices, check out Cas Solleric at no. 11 *(tel. 9 71 82 72 37 | €€)*. Afterwards, stroll down Carrer Major and explore the lovely shops such as the well-established pottery workshop Call Vermell at no. 44.

LIGHT UP YOUR DAY

The next destination is ❹ Portocolom ➤ p. 100, Felanitx's port. The funnel-shaped village is framed by colourfully painted boat sheds belonging to the fishermen. A visit to the somewhat hidden church square, Plaça Sant Jaume, is worth the effort because it shows you the most authentic side of the town. The village bars are the place to go to have a drink alongside the locals.

Before dinner, you should walk to the lighthouse, which is located on the Punta de Sa Cresta, *about 3km from the heart of the old village*. It separates the narrow bay from the wide, open sea and the view out over the Med is fantastic. It's an easy walk that will take less than a 30 minutes each way. Afterwards go to the harbour restaurant Sa Sinia *(Tue–Sun 1–3.30pm and 7.30–10.30pm | tel. 9 71 82 43 23 | €€€)* for supper. They serve delicious freshly caught fish. An inexpensive hotel at the beach is the Club Cala Marsal *(hotelclub calamarsal.com)*.

❸ Felanitx

15 km 35 mins

❹ Portocolom

30 km 1 hr 40 mins

The next morning, start your day by *driving into the first foothills of the Serra de Llevant*. Pass through the flower-bedecked villages of S'Horta and Calonge and, via S'Alquería Blanca ➤ p. 117, to the edge of Santanyí ➤ p. 114. Follow the road sign in the direction of Cala S'Amarador/Cala Mondragó.

INTO THE GENETS' TERRITORY

This road, as is typical for the south of the island, is lined by drystone walls *(parets seques)*. It comes to an end after *5km* at the gate to the nature reserve ⑤ Parc Natural Mondragó ➤ p. 117. The park is home to 70 bird species as well as rare plants and animals such as tortoises and genets. From the visitor centre, it is *about 500m on foot* through the fragrant pine forest to the beautiful bay of ⑥ Ses Fonts de n'Alís, which is a popular place to swim in summer.

⑤ Parc Natural Mondragó
1km 15 mins

⑥ Ses Fonts de n'Alís
0.6km 10 mins

A short *path along the rocky coast* leads to the other bay within the park, the ⑦ Cala S'Amarador. You only have to walk about 2.5km from here to get back to the car park. A narrow, *U-shaped trail* at the end of the Amarador beach heads through thick undergrowth and Mediterranean forests of juniper and pines. *It starts off to the side, to the right if you are looking at the sea*. Hike about half an hour to the rocky coastline and into the forest. *At the point where the path curves to the right, away from the sea,* the trail meets a *tarmac road* that you should *follow to the right* to get back to Amarador beach and return to the car park.

⑦ Cala S'Amarador
14km 1 hr

THE ROMANCE OF FISHING

On the way back to Santanyí, a road branches off to the left to the resort of ⑧ Cala Figuera ➤ p. 116, your next stop and the second fishing harbour on this route. In the afternoon, you can watch as the fishing boats return with their catch. *Stroll along the lovely Paseo Marítimo* high above the bay and stop off on the way back, for example at the Bon-Bar with its pretty view of the harbour. A good place to spend the night is Rocamar (rocamarplayamar.com). The hotel sits openly next to the sea and has its own path to the water.

⑧ Cala Figuera
20km 40 mins

A SHOWER IN THE SURF AT THE SOUTHERN TIP

The next day, try to get an early start and *head to Santanyí*, from where you need to *follow the signs to Colònia de Sant Jordi and Llombards*. Shortly past Llombards, *turn left on the Ma6110* and drive for 10km towards the southern tip of Mallorca. An easy hiking trail leads from the ❾ Cap de Ses Salines along the unspoilt coastline to the heavenly bay of ❿ Platja d'es Caragol (pack sun protection!). This beach, just like the neighbouring bay of Cala Entugores, is popular among nudists. Both beaches are among the most beautiful natural beaches on the island. Enjoy an unforgettable morning swim. It takes about half an hour on the path through the dunes, grass and sand to get there and back.

❾ **Cap de Ses Salines**
1.7km 25 mins

❿ **Platja d'es Caragol**
20km 45 mins

SKIM OFF A PINCH OF KNOWLEDGE

Once you're back at the car, *drive through Ses Salines* to the ⓫ Salines d'Es Trenc ➤ p. 119. The island is flat and mostly treeless around here. Only bird calls interrupt the silence of the salt pools. On a tour, you can learn interesting facts about the ecosystem of the wetlands with its many species and habitats as well as about how sea salt is harvested and produced; the process is tightly linked to the seasons of the year.

⓫ **Salines d'Es Trenc**
4.5km 5 mins

For a delicious lunch, head to ⓬ Colònia de Sant Jordi ➤ p. 118. The young chef at Sal de Cocó uses salt flakes from the coast in her dishes, many of which also feature freshly caught Mallorcan fish.

⓬ **Colònia de Sant Jordi**
9km 30 mins

STUNNING SEASIDE SUNSET

After lunch, *drive back towards the Salines d'Es Trenc*. The white mountains of salt and the pink/blue-grey evaporation pools sit just before the completely unspoilt beach of ⓭ Es Trenc ➤ p. 113, which has been saved through the efforts of a GOB (Grup Balear d'Ornitologia i Defensa de la Naturalesa) environmental initiative. Relax for the rest of the day between dunes reminiscent of the British North Sea coast and the turquoise-coloured waters of the crescent-shaped

⓭ **Es Trenc**
41km 50 mins

bay. As evening approaches, the bay becomes even more magical as the crowds disappear. On the way back, drive through Campos ➤ p. 111, Porreres ➤ p. 131 and Montuïri ➤ p. 130 to return to ❶ Sineu.

❶ Sineu

❹ A HIKE TO THE HERMITAGE OF BETLEM

➤ Tramp through fragrant rosemary and yellow gorse
➤ Experience total silence in the hermitage
➤ Have a dip in Colònia de Sant Pere

📍	Car park Ma3331 Artà-Betlem	🚩	Colònia de Sant Pere
→	10km	🥾	½ day (total walking time: 2½ hrs)
📶	moderate	↗	250m

ℹ The actual hike is only 7km long but is uphill all the way to the hermitage; you will need a car for the other 3km. The hermitage does not have a restaurant or residents. After walking back down, you can stop to eat in the small beach town of ❹ **Colònia de Sant Pere.**

At *Km7.5 on the Ma3331 country road*, which runs from Artà to Betlem, you will find a ❶ spot to park your car next to a broad path. The signs from there will direct you to the "Cases de Betlem, Ermita de Betlem, S'Alqueria Vella". The trail *heads past abandoned buildings and through the thorny brush* right into the mountains.

LISTEN TO THE BIRDS SING
The start of the walk is sunny and steep. After just a few metres, stop to enjoy the view of the bay of Alcúdia ➤ p. 85. Then the trail becomes a bit more strenuous. It curves upwards, *following the course of a*

❶ Car park
3.5km 1 hr 10 mins

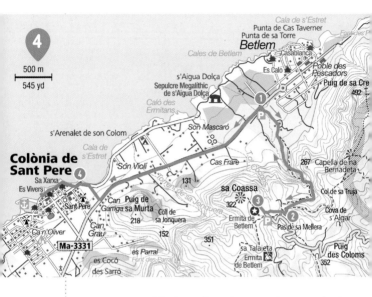

mountain stream, through gorse and rosemary bushes. The peninsula of the natural conservation area called the Parc de Llevant is uninhabited and largely unspoilt.

Later on, the trail *crosses through a valley* overshadowed by spectacular rocky crags. Then you will finally come to the pass, where it's an easy walk as you pass a spring, the ② Font de s'Ermita, and grotto dedicated to the Virgin Mary. Sit down and rest for a few minutes on the stone benches.

② Font de s'Ermita
0.5km 5 mins

SUBMERGE YOURSELF IN SILENCE

It only takes a few minutes to get to the ③ Hermitage ➤ p. 82 from here. Up until a few years ago, hermits still lived here and cared for the fruit orchards and vegetable gardens. Today, the house is uninhabited, but the monks in the nearby town of Artà ➤ p. 80 run the estate. Sheep and donkeys graze on the meadows that are filled with daisies in the spring. Light floods through the impressive church whose colourful rosette windows are worth a look. It is a place of absolute silence and wonderful for it.

③ Hermitage
6km 1 hr 10 mins

In the open valley surrounding the hermitage, you can take a nap on the grass or grab your binoculars and look for goats on the cliffs of the mountains or eagles flying overhead. When you've had your fill, *hike back downhill* to where your car is parked.

And then, for a quick stop for a cool off before heading home, make a detour to ❹ Colònia de Sant Pere ➤ p. 83 and take advantage of the lovely sandy beach for a late afternoon swim. Afterwards, treat yourself to a nice meal in one of the restaurants in this small, peaceful resort town, such as Sa Xarxa, which sits right next to the sea under tamarind trees.

INSIDER TIP
A dip in the sea is a must

❹ Colònia de Sant Pere

Find peace and tranquility at Ermita de Betlem

GOOD TO KNOW
HOLIDAY BASICS

ARRIVAL

Adaptor Type C

Two-pin European plug required.

GETTING THERE

International flights touch down at Palma de Mallorca (Son Sant Joan airport). Flight time from London is under 2.5 hours, and Palma is served by most UK regional airports. The majority of holidaymakers use budget airlines (prices vary wildly depending on when you book). Scheduled economy-class flights with BA or Iberia are generally more expensive, although they are now trying to be more competitive.

Several car-hire firms tout for business at the airport; taxis offer transfers to the island's other regions and towns. The longest trip, to Cala Rajada, costs about 90 euros; to central Palma around 25 euros. Normal, scheduled buses travel from the airport to Palma *(departures every 15 mins | journey time 25 mins | ticket 5 euros)* and to many coastal resorts as well *(5–12 euros | tib.org).*

Travelling from London to Mallorca by car involves about 1,100km of motorway driving, via Orléans, Bourges, Clermond-Ferrand, Millau and Barcelona. Toll charges in France and Spain easily add up to over 100 euros.

Travel time from London to Barcelona on sleeper or daytime trains is about 15 hours. Depending on the season, a regular second-class return ticket from London starts at around 150 euros (but can be more). The website *www.seat61.com* is excellent for timetables and ticketing links. Keep an eye out for special offers.

The ferry companies *Baleària*

Getting to the Torrent de Pareis is all part of the experience

(balearia.com) and *Acciona Trasmediterránea (trasmediterranea.com)* connect Mallorca to the mainland ports of Barcelona, Valencia and Dénia. The severn-hour crossing (car and two adults return) costs around 500 euros. Specialist travel agencies for these crossings include *www.aferry.com, www.ocean24.de* and *www.direct ferries.com.*

GETTING IN

Since Brexit, long queues have been reported at immigration in Spanish airports. Make sure you have enough time left on your passport when arriving in Spain (and that you have the correct visa should you need one – i.e. for longer trips).

CLIMATE & WHEN TO GO

The north is cooler than the south. Spring is usually mild with cool evenings and rain showers. Summers are hot with occasional storms. August has high levels of humidity. Autumn stays warm well into October, after that the first cold spells arrive, and with them a lot of precipitation. Winters are predominantly mild, and due to high humidity in the evening and at night, it gets a lot colder. High season is from May to October, although many tourists also come for the almond blossom season in January/February or in the Easter holidays.

GETTING AROUND

RULES OF THE ROAD

Apart from driving on the right-hand side of the road, traffic regulations are broadly similar to the UK. Maximum speed limits on motorways: 120kmh;

on country roads: 90kmh. Seat belts have to be worn at all times, and a helmet must be worn on all motorised two-wheel vehicles. The blood alcohol limit is strict at 0.5g per litre. Carrying two fluorescent vests and two warning triangles is compulsory, and using a mobile phone whilst driving is prohibited. Fines *(multas)* are high (sometimes more than 100 euros). Just as in the UK, if you pay your fine right away or within a few days, you'll receive a discount of up to 50 per cent, depending on the municipality.

In villages and towns, blue lines signify limited and payable parking, yellow ones signal no parking. Ignore parking restrictions at your peril unless you want to pay *multas* or have your car towed away. In the blue parking zones in the centre of Palma, you have to get a pay-and-display ticket at the machine for 120 to 180 minutes. If you exceed that time, you risk a wheel clamp or will even be towed away. You'll have unlimited parking time in the expensive multistorey car parks in the capital, but you need to get there early in the morning; later on in the day, Palma, the city with the highest traffic density in Spain, will be jam-packed.

CAR HIRE

During peak season, hundreds of car-hire companies offer around 60,000 rental cars. Compare deals: particularly cheap offers aren't necessarily the most trustworthy. It is worth taking out fully comprehensive insurance with no excess in case of damage. A hire car of the lower category costs about 175 euros a week excluding petrol – when you book from home that is. Generally hire cars booked over the internet from home (from and to the airport) are a lot cheaper than those rented on a whim in the airport or at a resort.

FERRIES

If you want to do some island hopping, *Baleària (www.balearia.com)* ferries depart from Alcúdia and take you to Menorca in about 90 minutes; from Palma, they reach Ibiza in about four hours. Formentera can only be reached by ferry from Ibiza. Apart from Baleària, *Acciona Trasmediterránea (www.trasmediterranea.es)* also operates inter-island services.

MARINAS

A list of all Balearic marinas, with information on location, size, number of moorings, maximum length of boats allowed and port facilities, as well as of all providers of charter yachts, can be obtained from *Mallorca nautic (Paseo Marítimo 16a | Palma | tel. 9 71 28 00 07 | mallorcanautic.com)*.

PUBLIC TRANSPORT

The underground bus and railway station in Palma is called Estació Intermodal *(below the park opposite Plaça Espanya)*. This is where the trains to Inca–Muro–Sa Pobla or Inca–Sineu–Monacor and all overland buses to all towns on the island leave from. There is an information point with English-speaking staff. The Balearic regional transport authority *TIB (tel. 9 71 17 77 77 | tib.org)* provides information

FESTIVALS & EVENTS
ALL YEAR ROUND

JANUARY/FEBRUARY

Eve of Sant Antoni (in Palma, Sa Pobla, Andratx and other): *Dimonis* (devils) cause havoc while priests praise animals from horses to goldfish.

Almond Blossom Festival (Son Servera): see p. 104. *calamillor.com,*

MARCH/APRIL

Day of the Balearic Islands (Palma harbour): medieval-themed festival.

Semana Santa/Pasqua: At 7pm on Maundy Thursday the biggest procession of masked fraternities starts in Palma. On Good Friday, for *Devallament*, fraternities from Pollença carry a statue of Christ from "Calvary" into the church.

MAY/JUNE

Fira (Sóller): Recreation of the battle between Moors and Christians that took place in 1561.

Processó de les Aguiles (Pollença): Two beautifully decked-out girls in eagle costumes lead the procession.

International Jazz Festival (Cala d'Or): *visitcalador.com*

Octopus festival (Portocolom)

Medieval Market (Capdepera): *feriamedieval.es*

Herb fair (Selva): *firadesesherbes.com*

JULY/AUGUST

Concert in Torrent de Pareis (Escorca): classical music with a stunning backdrop *ajescorca.net.*

Festival Chopin (Valldemossa): *festivalchopin.com*

SEPTEMBER/OCTOBER

Nit de l'Art (Palma): a night for art-lovers, see p. 50. *nitdelartartpalma.com*

Sweet festival (Esporles): *ajesporles. net*

NOVEMBER/DECEMBER

Dijous Bo (Inca): largest harvest market on the island. *dijousbo.es*

Christmas Market (Palma): in Plaça Major and in Pueblo Espanyol.

about connections, timetables and prices in multiple languages on its website or by telephone. Tickets can be bought from the driver – make sure you have enough small change.

Near the Estació Intermodal you will find the Art Nouveau railway station serving the nostalgic *Ferrocarril de Sóller*. There are few connections between other towns on the island; everything centres around Palma.

You can hire bikes at the station – apart from the historic quarter and in the entirely pedestrianised areas, a bike is not a bad way to get around Palma, and it's green to boot!

EMERGENCIES

CONSULATES AND EMBASSIES
British Consulate
C/ Convent dels Caputxins | 4 Edificio Orisba B 4° | Palma | tel. 9 33 66 62 00 | ukinspain.fco.gov.uk/en
Irish consulate general
San Miguel, 68 | Palma | tel. 9 71 71 92 44
US consulate agency
Porto Pi, 8 | Palma | tel. 9 71 40 37 07

EMERGENCY NUMBER
Call 112 for the police, fire service and ambulance.

HEALTH
The island has a comprehensive network of doctors' surgeries (you'll find addresses of English-speaking medics in the *Majorca Daily Bulletin* available from newsstands) and pharmacies

(farmacias). There are also 11 private and 10 state-run hospitals. If you need to visit a doctor or hospital, an interpreter will be provided, so don't worry about your Catalan/Spanish skills.

INSIDER TIP
Don't worry about the language barrier

Over a dozen alternative medicine providers have settled on Mallorca. The holiday resorts have their own *centros médicos*, and the Red Cross *(Cruz Roja)* provides first aid on many beaches.

ESSENTIALS

BANKS
Practically all towns on the island have several banks, and there are few places without an ATM cash machine.

BOAT TOURS
Boats ahoy! If you take a 🐵 boat tour with real fishermen, you will have a great day out getting to see how the fishing industry works and, if you are in luck, you may see dolphins. *Pescaturismo Mallorca (prices from 75 euros, children are half price | pesca turismomallorca.com)* run trips for the whole family from a total of 13 harbours including Palma, Port d'Andratx and Port de Sóller.

CAMPSITES
Wild camping (outside a campsite) is forbidden but, if you call ahead, you can pitch your tent at the *Lluc Monastery (200 spaces | showers,*

drinking water) or in the *Es Pixarells* compound *(24 spaces | toilet, drinking water | Ctra. Lluc–Escorca)*. Both campsites are open throughout the year *(tel. 9 71 51 70 70 for reservations)*. The campsite *S'Arenalet (20 spaces | toilets, showers, drinking water | Ctra. Artà–Cala Torta | tel. 9 71 17 76 52 | refugis@ibanat.caib.es | closed Jan)* is beautifully located on the unspoilt coast of Artà. Individual hikers can call the league for the protection of birds, *GOB (C/ Manuel Sanchis Guarner 10 | Palma | tel. 9 71 49 60 60)* and camp out in their site *La Trapa (Andratx | can only be reached on foot | 4 spaces | all year)*, located in the mountains with a great view of the sea and the island of Dragonera. The *Hipocampo* site *(C/ Es Domingos Vells | Cales de Mallorca | tel. 9 71 83 37 15 | clubhipocampo.com)* is located on the east coast. They offer a large communal hut for groups alongside individual pitches.

CUSTOMS

EU citizens can import and export goods for their personal use tax-free (800 cigarettes, 1kg tobacco, 90 litres of wine, 10 litres of spirits over 22 % vol.). Visitors from other countries must observe the following limits, except for items for personal use. Duty free: max. 50 g perfume, 200 cigarettes, 50 cigars, 250g tobacco, 1 litre of spirits (over 22 % vol.), 2 litres of spirits (under 22 % vol.), 2 litres of any wine.

ECO TOURISM TAX

Visitors to Mallorca have to pay a visitor's tax, the Ecotasa, the earnings of which are supposed to promote sustainable tourism. It is payable by every guest over 16 and is based on the number of nights you stay. Tourists arriving on Mallorca on a cruise ship have to pay as well. In peak season *(May to October)* you'll have to pay between 1 and 4 euros per day plus VAT, depending on the category of your accommodation. In the low season, it's half that amount. If you stay ten days or longer, you'll get a reduction. The tax is collected at the hotel's reception desk or by the landlord of your finca or holiday flat.

FOREST FIRES

There isn't that much forest on Mallorca in the first place, which is why forest fires, often occurring after extended periods of hot weather and drought, can have a dramatic impact. Don't ever throw a cigarette butt out of a driving car, don't leave any glass bottles lying around and don't start a barbecue in the forest – there are hefty fines!

INTERNET & WIFI

Many cafés and restaurants offer their customers free WiFi. Most bars share their network with the customers if you ask for the password. Mallorca is working to establish Europe's largest wireless network; it already offers 300 WiFi hotspots *(mallorca-wifi)*. Places with unrestricted internet access in Palma include the Platja de Palma, the old jetty, the Parc de la Mar and the subterranean bus terminal on the Plaça Espanya.

MEDIA

Nearly all hotels offer British and other English-language TV programmes via satellite. Newsstands and kiosks sell British newspapers, as well as local English-language daily, weekly and monthly papers and magazines, such as *Majorca Daily Bulletin*, *Dígame* or *Euro Weekly News*. The English-language island radio *(www.radio onemallorca.com)* broadcasts 24/7 on 105.6 FM.

NATIONAL HOLIDAYS

1 Jan	New Year's Day
6 Jan	Epiphany
1 March	*Dia de les Illes Balears*
	(Balearic regional holiday)
late March/April	Easter
1 May	Labour Day
25 July	*Fiesta Sant Jaume*
15 Aug	Assumption
12 Oct	*Dia de l'Hispanitat*
	(Discovery of America Day)
1 Nov	All Saints' Day
6 Dec	*Dia de la Constitució* (Constitution Day)
8 Dec	Immaculate Conception
25/26 Dec	Christmas

OPENING HOURS

Restaurants are usually open *1–4pm and 7.30–11pm*, shops on weekdays *9am–1/1.30pm, 4–8.30pm and later*. It's becoming more and more common for shops and bars to work through the afternoon without a lunchtime siesta.

PHONES & MOBILE PHONES

Using hotel telephones is very expensive. For calls outside Spain dial 00 followed by the dialling code for the country (UK 44, Ireland 353, US and Canada 1), then the number of the person you are calling. The code for Spain is 0034. Spanish telephone numbers consist of nine digits and there are no local area codes. Mallorcan landlines begin with 971 or (occasionally) 871 while mobile numbers begin with a 6 or (occasionally) 7.

POST

Stamps can be bought from the post office *(correos)* and in the tobacco shops *(tabaco, estanco)*. Letterboxes are yellow. Post stamped with private firms' stamps will only be collected from that particular company's letterbox.

PRICES

The prices on Mallorca are similar to those in the rest of Europe. The weekly markets are not bazaars and haggling over prices is uncommon. Fresh meat continues to be good value; fresh fish less so, as it has become rare here too. Tourists complain about high prices in restaurants – rightly so in many places, especially as prices often seem to bear little relation to the quality. A bottle of table wine costing some 2.50 euros in the supermarket can cost 15 times as much in a restaurant. Organised trips are also a drain on holiday finances: 30–65 euros for a day trip without packed lunch or for a show evening with a set menu.

TIPPING

Anybody working in the service industry is glad of a tip. In restaurants, it is customary to add up to 10 per cent to

HOW MUCH DOES IT COST?

Taxi	from 0.88 euros *per kilometre*
Bike hire	from 10 euros *per day*
Coffee	from 1.40 euros *for an espresso*
Beach	12–15 euros *for two recliners with parasol*
Tapas	from 3.50 euros *for a small portion*
Ice cream	from 1.50 euros *for a scoop*

the total bill. Hotel maids expect 5–6 euros at the end of a week's stay. The charge for taxis or private coach transport should be rounded up generously, and guides usually receive a gratuity of at least 5–10 euros or more if you were happy with the service.

TOURIST INFORMATION
spain.info
UK: 64 North Row | London W1K 7DE | tel. 020 7317 2011
Both the Balearic Island government tourist information website *(illes balears.travel)* and the Mallorca island council tourist information website *(infomallorca.net)* are available in four languages (including English). Virtually every town has a tourist information office where the staff usually speak good English. The most centrally located one in Palma is on the Plaça de la Reina.

WEATHER

High season
Low season

	JAN	FEB	MARCH	APRIL	MAY	JUNE	JULY	AUG	SEPT	OCT	NOV	DEC
Daytime temperatures in °C	14°	15°	17°	19°	23°	27°	29°	30°	27°	23°	18°	15°
Night time temperatures in °C	6°	6°	7°	9°	13°	16°	19°	19°	18°	14°	10°	7°
☀ Sunshine hours/day	5	6	6	7	10	10	11	11	8	6	5	5
🌂 Rainy days/month	6	6	6	4	4	2	1	2	5	6	7	7
≋ Sea temperatures in °C	14°	13°	14°	15°	17°	21°	24°	25°	24°	21°	18°	15°

☀ Sunshine hours/day   🌂 Rainy days/month   ≋ Sea temperatures in °C

USEFUL PHRASES
CATALAN

SMALLTALK

Yes/no/maybe	sí/no/potser
Please	sisplau
Thank you	gràcies
Hello!/Good afternoon/evening/night	Hola!/Bon dia!/Bona tarda!/ Bona nit!
Goodbye	Adéu! Passi-ho bé!
My name is	Em dic …
What is your name? (formal/informal)	Com es diu?/Com et dius?
I am from	Sóc de …
Excuse me/sorry!	Perdona!/Perdoni!
Pardon/Could you repeat? (formal/ informal)	Com diu?/Com dius?
I (don't) like this	(No) m'agrada.
I would like/do you have?	Voldria …/Té …?
May I?	Puc …?

SYMBOLS

EATING & DRINKING

Could I please have…?	**Podria portar-me …?**
Knife/fork/spoon	**ganivet/forquilla/cullera**
Salt/pepper/sugar	**sal/pebrot/sucre**
Vinegar/oil	**vinagre/oli**
Milk/cream/lemon	**llet/crema de llet/llimona**
With/without ice/gas (in water)	**amb/sense gel/gas**
Cold/over-seasoned/undercooked	**fred/salat/cru**
Could we have the bill please?	**El compte, sisplau.**
Bill/receipt	**compte/rebut**
Tip	**propina**
In cash/by card	**al comptat/amb targeta de crèdit**

MISCELLANEOUS

Where is…/Where are…?	**On està …?/On estan …?**
What time is it?	**Quina hora és?**
Today/tomorrow/yesterday	**avui/demà/ahir**
How much is…?	**Quant val …?**
Where can I find Internet/WiFi?	**On em puc connectar a Internet/WLAN?**
Can I take a photo of you/here?	**Puc fer-li una foto aquí?**
Help! Watch out!	**Ajuda!/Compte!**
Broken	**trencat**
Broken down/garage	**avaria/taller**
Pharmacy/chain drug store	**farmàcia/drogueria**
Temperature/pain	**febre/dolor**
Timetable/ticket	**horario/bitllet**
Ban/banned	**prohibició/prohibit**
Open/closed	**obert/tancat**
Right/left/straight on	**a la dreta/a l'esquerra/tot recte**
More/less	**més/menys**
Cheap/expensive	**barat/car**
Not/drinking water	**aigua (no) potable**
0/1/2/3/4/5/6/7/8/9/10/100/1000	**zero/un, una/dos, dues/tres/quatre/cinc/sis/set/vuit/nou/deu/cent/mil**

HOLIDAY VIBES

FOR RELAXATION & CHILLING

FOR BOOKWORMS & FILM BUFFS

📖 A WINTER IN MALLORCA

This wonderful book tells of the love-hate relationship that George Sand had with the island and its inhabitants in the winter of 1838-39, a visit she experienced – and suffered – with her lover Frédéric Chopin in Palma and Valldemossa. Descriptions of places still seem very accurate to this day, although the book was first published in 1842.

📖 THE VACATIONERS

Emma Straub's novel (2014) is set during a hot summer in a remote holiday home at the foot of the Tramuntana mountains where a rather dysfunctional extended family spends

their holidays and all family members face problems of their own.

📖 PEACOCKS IN PARADISE

Anna Nicholas has been living on Mallorca for a long time and she writes crime novels set on the island. More of a travelogue (contains tips too), *Peacocks in Paradise* is a charming and accessible way to get to understand the island better.

🎥 CLOUD ATLAS

Halle Berry, Tom Hanks, Hugh Grant and Mallorca's amazing scenery: Sa Calobra, Sóller and Puig Major served as the setting for most of the filming of David Mitchell's novel (2012).

PLAYLIST

0:58

|| MARIA DEL MAR BONET – LA BALANGUERA
Mallorca's anthem, sung with great emotion by this Mallorcan singer.

▶ FRANCISCO FULLANA – FOUR SEASONS RECOMPOSED, SPRING
A stunningly talented violinist who is on the way to being a global star. He was born in Palma.

▶ TOMEU PENYA – ÉS PER TU
Part of the island's furniture, this songwriter and singer has sung folk, rock and country.

▶ POSIDÒNIA FOLK MEDITERRANI – LLUNA
A six-part folk band that plays an interesting mix of styles.

▶ DAVID GÓMEZ – THE ISLAND
A pianist and composer who is known to give concerts in amazing locations on the island.

Your holiday soundtrack can be found on **Spotify** under **MARCO POLO** Spain

Or scan this code with the Spotify app

ONLINE

MOBIPALMA
Car parks, taxi ranks, bike hire, buses (and where they stop) up-to-date traffic reports, charging points for electric cars. All of this and much more is to be found on this free Palma app.

FARSDEBALEARS.ORG
Lighthouses! Incredible photos and panoramic images of these majestic structures. Audio guides in English too.

TAPAS PALMA
For all of those who like their portions small, this app will tell you when a tapas tour is happening. For example,

the Molinar and Portixol weekly Wednesday restaurant crawls.

WALKINGONWORDS.COM
Tours which link places on the island to famous literary figures. As Gertrude Stein once said "Mallorca is a paradise if you can stand it." Also available as an app: WOW! Mallorca.

PLATGESDEBALEARS.COM
A website about beaches run by the Balearic government. If you fancy a quick trip to Menorca, Ibiza or Formentera while you are here, this is the place to do your beach research.

TRAVEL PURSUIT
THE MARCO POLO HOLIDAY QUIZ

Have you worked out what makes Mallorca tick? Use this quiz to test your knowledge of the island's customs and quirks. You'll find the answers at the bottom of the page, with further information on pages 18–23.

❶ What used be to smuggled around Mallorca on a network of secret paths?
a) Cigarettes, alcohol and coffee
b) Valuable coins from Roman and Phoenician archaeological sites
c) Eggs belonging to the rare Balearic lizard, coveted by zoos across Europe

❷ "The Balearic Islands in Words and Images" is …
a) A great retro TV series, which is back in fashion
b) The famous book written by the Austrian archduke, Ludwig Salvator
c) The latest app produced by the Balearic government

❸ Why are there different ways of writing place names on the island?
a) Because the local government can never decide what sounds better
b) Because no-one can be bothered to change old typos
c) Because there are two official languages

❹ Mallorcans used to use sling-shots to throw stones. But why?
a) Island people are often a bit nuts
b) It was a way to fight off invaders
c) There were simply so many hanging around

Lluc Alcari enjoys a stunning position on the west coast

❺ What are the huge birds called which circle above the Tramuntana?
a) Black vultures
b) Giant blackbirds
c) Herons

❻ Ramon Llull is famous in many parts of the world. But why?
a) He was a particularly dangerous fighter who could "lull" his opponents into a false sense of security
b) He was the equivalent of Shakespeare to the island
c) Because as a Republican he continues to protest against the Spanish royal family

❼ What are talaiots?
a) The first currency on the island
b) What priests wear on Mallorca
c) Prehistoric structures

❽ What is Neptune grass good for?
a) It is the favourite food of Neptune, the God of the Sea
b) It serves as a playground for baby fish
c) Nothing. It is just an underwater weed

❾ What are the other Balearic Islands called?
a) La Palma, La Gomera and Fuerteventura
b) Ibiza, Sardinia and Formentera
c) Ibiza, Menorca and Formentera

❿ Mallorca has something which has been awarded UNESCO World Heritage status. But what?
a) The Tramuntana mountains
b) The party scene
c) The unspoilt beach, Es Trenc

INDEX

WE WANT TO HEAR FROM YOU!

Did you have a great holiday? Is there something on your mind? Whatever it is, let us know! Whether you want to praise the guide, alert us to errors or give us a personal tip – MARCO POLO would be pleased to hear from you. Please contact us by email.

We do everything we can to provide the very latest information for your trip. Nevertheless, despite all of our authors' thorough research, errors can creep in. MARCO POLO does not accept any liability for this.

e-mail: sales@heartwoodpublishing.co.uk

PICTURE CREDITS

Cover photo: Cala S'Almonia near Santanyi (Schapowalow: H. - P. Huber)
Photos: DuMont Bildarchiv: F. Heuer (14/15, 30/31, 61, 68, 81, 88, 103), Schwarzbach (34, 155); R. Hackenberg (93); huber-images: G. Croppi (62), C. Dörr (front flap outside, front flap inside, 1), H. - P. Huber (164/165), Molina (74/75), R. Schmid (11, 24/25, 38/39, 43, 132), C. Seba (back flap); Laif: M. Gonzalez (8, laif: M. Gonzalez (27, Laif: M. Gonzalez (54, 124, 129); laif: Heuer (100); Laif: F. Heuer (112, 126); laif: Th. Linkel (47); Laif: J. Modrow (116); Laif/hemis.fr: L. Maisant (49); laif/Le Figaro Magazine: Fautre (142); laif/Zenit: P. Langrock (134/135); K. Lehmkuhl (167); Look: T. Roetting (22), Roetting/Pollex (152/153); Look/age fotostock (111); mauritius images: S. Beuthan (82), M. Habel (2/3, 94/95), D. Kempf-Seifried (162), M. Lange (98, 120/121), E. Wrba (26/27, 139), mauritius images/age (32/33, 64); mauritius images/age fotostock: S. Torrens (85); mauritius images/Alamy (9, 10); mauritius images/Alamy live news: J. Llado (12/13); mauritius images/Alamy: A. - M. Palmer (44), J. Power (105), Vulcano (131); mauritius images/Alamy/Panther Media GmbH (78/79, 119); mauritius images/Alamy/PBpictures (106/107); mauritius images/Axiom Photographic: I. Cumming (50/51); mauritius images/Imagebroker (146); mauritius images/imagebroker: M. Moxter (72); mauritius images/John WarburtonLee: D. Pearson (20); mauritius images/Westend61: M. Moxter (6/7, 56/57); picture-alliance/dpa (151); vario images/Westend61 (19); E. Wrba (31)

4th Edition – fully revised and updated 2022
Worldwide Distribution: Heartwood Publishing Ltd, Bath, United Kingdom
www.heartwoodpublishing.co.uk

© MAIRDUMONT GmbH & Co. KG, Ostfildern
Author: Kirsten Lehmkuhl, Petra Rossbach
Editor: Franziska Kahl, Felix Wolf
Picture editor: Gabriele Forst
Cartography: © MAIRDUMONT, Ostfildern (pp. 36–37, 136, 141, 145, 150, outer flap, pull-out map) © MAIRDUMONT, Ostfildern, using data from OpenStreetMap, Licence CC-BY-SA 2.0 (pp. 40-41, 53, 58-59, 66, 71, 76-77, 86, 90, 96-97, 108-109, 115, 122-123).
Cover design and pull-out map design: bilekjaeger_Kreativagentur with Zukunftswerkstatt, Stuttgart
Page design: Langenstein Communication GmbH, Ludwigsburg

Heartwood Publishing credits:
Translated from the German by John Owen, Kathleen Becker, Jennifer Walcoff Neuheiser, Suzanne Kirkbright
Editors: Felicity Laughton, Kate Michell, Sophie Blacksell Jones
Prepress: Summerlane Books, Bath
Printed in India

MARCO POLO AUTHOR
KIRSTEN LEHMKUHL

The author always thought Mallorca was too brash and too busy for her until she attended a language course in Palma. It was love at first sight: the cathedral, the sea, the atmospheric old town ... She decided to stay and has since spent 20 years living and working as a journalist and media manager in both Germany and Mallorca.

DOS & DON'TS

HOW TO AVOID SLIP-UPS & BLUNDERS

DON'T SWIM TOO FAR OUT

The sea may look very calm but looks can be deceiving. The Mediterranean has lots of underwater currents which can make it very difficult to get back to land. Don't go further than you can stand and never swim if a red flag is up!

DON'T WASTE WATER

Water is a valuable resource on the island and its groundwater levels are dangerously low. There are desalination plants but these are pretty bad for the environment.

DON'T TOUCH JELLYFISH

These blobby creatures can cause really nasty stings. If you do happen to touch one in the water, clean the area with salt water (fresh water won't work). You can also use anti-irritant creams for mosquito bites or ice packs to lessen the pain. Look out for warning signs on the beach: a white flag with a purple jellyfish.

DO BE PREPARED IN THE MOUNTAINS

You may think nothing bad can happen in the Tramuntana but you'd be wrong! Every year there are numerous accidents there. Make sure you have decent shoes, a hat, sun cream and enough water. And take a guide (a book or a person)!

DO GET CHANGED BEFORE GETTING ON THE BUS

Most tourist hotspots now have codes of conduct for tourists. Obvious binge drinking is banned, as is urinating in public and causing too much noise. Most codes also say you cannot travel on public transport wearing your swimming gear, so wrap up or get changed before boarding.